JOANNA SHEEN

THE MICROWAVE
Pressed Flower
MANUAL

AURUM PRESS

First published in Great Britain
1998 by Aurum Press Limited
25 Bedford Avenue, London WC1B 3AT

Photographs by Di Lewis and
David Johnson

A catalogue record for this book is available from the British Library.

ISBN 1 85410 483 7

1 3 5 7 9 10 8 6 4 2
1998 2000 2002 2001 1999

Applemac design by Kit Johnson
with Dorchester Typesetting Group Ltd

Printed in Hong Kong / China
by South China Printing Co. (1988) Ltd

Contents

Introduction

Pressing flowers has been a fascinating hobby for many people over the last hundred years. The main drawback has always been the need to wait patiently while the flowers dry in the presses for six to eight weeks. But, with today's technology, you can take a short cut, achieve better, brighter results and use the flowers almost instantly. I actually recommend waiting overnight, but in times of desperation you can use the flowers or leaves the same day. What a difference to the time scale for making pictures! I hope that this increased speed in pressing will attract more young people to this fascinating hobby, and extend everyone's enjoyment of pressed flowers.

I have been working with pressed flowers for nearly twenty years now and during that time, one of my greatest fascinations has been travelling around the world learning about the different ways each country uses pressed flowers. There is a great tradition in many countries for decorating and creating with pressed flowers and I never fail to learn something new with every visit I make. Once you are 'hooked' on flower pressing, there seems to be no end to the ways in which the pressed bits and pieces can be used.

With this new microwave technique, there are hundreds more varieties that will press successfully. Microwave technology has the same effect on flower preservation as cookery – you have to start again from the beginning as it is a totally different technique that requires a little time and effort to get it right. I remember my first attempts at microwave cookery being somewhat disastrous, and the same can apply to microwave flower pressing. Take time to practise, try new varieties of flowers and always record everything as your own microwave will have different results to someone else's.

Don't let the inexactitudes of microwave technology put you off – this technique is exciting, quick and very rewarding. Once you have mastered it you will find you get successful results time after time. As the results are so immediate, your enthusiasm doesn't have time to wane. There are also many species of plant which do not preserve well with the traditional methods of pressing but do magnificently with the microwave technique. Orchids, for instance – the old methods gave a rather fierce brown colour, but in a microwave you can keep the softest gentlest greens, pinks, creams and even brilliant white.

So read the instructions carefully and then have a go! Remember that all microwaves tend to be a little different. We use three for our commercial pressing and they all need slightly different times and heats, so a little experimentation will probably be necessary. I hope that this book will fire your imagination with new ways to preserve, new plants to try and most of all new projects to make once you have your beautifully pressed flowers!

JOANNA SHEEN

CHAPTER 1

Flowers that Last

When you have arranged some fresh flowers in a stunning and wonderful display, it is disappointing to think that they will last only a short time. With new flower foods and the quality often available today your arrangement may last a good week – maybe two. But if you are busy working all day, that still doesn't give you much time to admire your handiwork. The best thing about pressed flowers is that they will last for many weeks, months and even years – depending upon the strength of the light they are exposed to and on other prevailing conditions, such as humidity.

One of the most rewarding things about having flower pressing as a hobby is that it enables you to study the flower – every small part of it – at leisure. When you are picking and arranging flowers *en masse* in a jug, you don't often stop to admire the reverse of a flowerhead, or the underside of a leaf, or the fascination of a tightly-furled bud. Pressing gives you time to do so and indeed leads you to look at nature in much greater detail as you preserve it and then use it artistically or decoratively.

Pressing flowers is by no means a new hobby – it has been popular in many countries for the last century at least. In Britain, Queen Victoria was a great exponent of the art and many Victorian ladies wandered along Britain's country lanes, collecting flowers as botanical specimens and pressing them. The whole language of flowers that developed in the Victorian era could then be used with preserved flowers as well as fresh. The Victorians were incurably romantic and many a flower presented to a young lady by an admirer was pressed between the pages of the heavy family Bible and sighed over at some later date.

Many of us are still incurably romantic and pressing flowers is a lovely way to preserve memories of happy occasions. Later in the book, you will find projects that use wedding flowers or flowers given to a mother on the birth of a new baby. Many sentimental occasions are marked with a gift of flowers, and what nicer memento of the occasion than a pressed flower picture or project made with those flowers.

Until now, the craft of pressed flowers has always entailed huge amounts of patience, and indeed the larger, more complex pressed flower pictures always will. However, in this book I have tried to bring a more contemporary, carefree approach to the use of pressed flowers by decorating with them and then covering them with varnish.

It takes much less skill and patience to decorate a plant pot with a few flowerheads and then varnish it, than it does to make up a complex picture design where every component must be in the right place to a tolerance of a few millimetres. Anyone can try decorating with pressed flowers; my children have experimented with the technique with great success and will vouch for the fact that it is quick, easy and great fun to do.

Another bonus of flower pressing is that it can be a relatively inexpensive hobby. Nowadays, everything seems to cost vast amounts and finding a hobby that doesn't require a huge outlay is often a difficult task. If you press flowers from your own garden they cost nothing. The most popular thing you could make with pressed flowers is a personalized birthday card. Everyone is immensely flattered if someone spends time and effort on making them a card, and a pressed flower card will probably be treasured long after the commercial ones have been thrown away. The cost for a project like that need only be the price of the paper and the glue.

WHAT TO PRESS?

Using this new microwave technique, there is probably no limit to the range of flower that you can press, but undoubtedly some varieties are more successful than others. It takes so little time just to pop a couple of flowers into the microwave press that it may be worth trying anything and everything – don't take no for an answer unless you have tried a couple of times and failed with a particular flower or leaf.

Take care to make full use of either a separate record book or the record sheets at the back of this book, to note the times and heats you have used for particular plants, and where you have found them. If a flower has come from your own garden then you may well remember where it is when you wish to pick some more. But, believe me, when the fever to pick and press overtakes you and you are raiding the gardens of friends and family, it is all too easy to forget completely where and when you found a certain plant! This can be extremely frustrating when you find that it presses beautifully and you decide you need just a few more stems to complete the most wonderful project in the world. So notes and records are very useful.

The lists of flowers given in this section of the book are to be used as a guideline. You need not confine yourself to these suggestions; try anything to which you have easy access. In many cases I may not list all varieties exhaustively as that can become boring and repetitive. For example, I have listed one variety of lily but it is worth trying any variety that you have to hand; the same applies to orchids, roses and foliage. I am not promising you equal success with all colours and varieties – that certainly varies – but it is worth trying.

WHAT TO LOOK FOR

Pressing flowers in the microwave is not a miracle process; if you put poor material in, you will get equally poor results. It is vitally important to press flowers that are at their peak or just reaching their peak of beauty. Flowers that are past their best will not keep such good colour or shape when they are preserved.

If you are picking flowers from a garden, try to pick only those that have just come into bloom that day. If the flower has already been blooming for a couple of days, the colour will have faded, the centre will be dull and the lasting qualities of the flower's colour will have diminished. Small ballerina roses, for example, have a brilliant yellow centre when they are newly in bloom; this gradually turns brown and the pink colour in the petals becomes lighter and lighter – all in the course of twenty-four hours.

It is not always easy to tell how long a flower has been blooming, but a detailed look at the centre may well furnish you with an answer. Even the modest little lawn daisy has a much tighter pretty centre when it is very new than a day or so later. If you have several flowers blooming on the same plant, compare them and you will soon be able to tell which are the newer blooms and which are the older ones.

Never pick flowers that have been nibbled by an enthusiastic insect or animal. A nibbled pansy that goes into the microwave press will come out as a beautifully pressed nibbled pansy. The only exception to this rule is when you are desperate for a few more flowers to complete a particular project and they may be tucked in an inconspicuous place where the nibbles won't show. Any sign of disease on a flower or leaf will still be visible once it has been pressed and it seems a shame to waste your time and electricity on a specimen that may well be doomed from the start.

If you are picking specimens from your own garden, the very best way to do it is little and often. Rather than picking absolutely everything that you want and then leaving some flowers to curl up or wilt while you are processing others, pick a few items and press them. You can always nip outside and pick a few more while the microwave is ticking over and 'cooking' your last batch of material.

If, however, you are collecting flowers from a friend's garden or while out for a walk (see Table of Suitable Flowers for notes on preferable wild flower varieties), then you will need to preserve the flowers as carefully as possible before transporting them home. I usually keep the shallow lid from a shoe box or something similar in the car, with a supply of polythene bags and tape. If you use the box lid as a tray, the flowers can be laid out on that and then slid into a polythene bag and taped up.

If you then leave this package in a hot or sunny position the flowers will die in minutes, so make sure that you place it in the coolest possible position out of the sun and aim to process the flowers as quickly as possible once you are home. This assumes that you have snipped off the flowerheads only; should you be lucky enough to have stems, them keep them in water or soaked cotton wool for as long as possible, still in a cool shady place. Obviously flowers on stems in water will last longer than individual flowerheads. However, a few flowerheads are less visible and may not damage a garden display as much as chopping off a lot of flowers complete with fine long stems.

It is worth thanking your friends enthusiastically and taking care not to overdo the number of flowers that you take when they have let you loose in their garden as they will then happily let you come back for more. Over-enthusiastic stripping of plants in a friend's garden could lead to invitations for late night drinks only – once it's dark and you are safe to have around!

FLOWERS FROM THE FLORIST

With traditional pressing methods, many commercially grown flowers were difficult to press and gave disappointing results. This new microwave pressing technique means there are so many more flowers from the florist that can be pressed successfully.

All roses press beautifully in the microwave, although the colour does change a little in some varieties, although far less noticeably than with a traditional press. As with all multi-petalled flowers, you will have to dismantle the flower and press it petal by petal to get excellent results. The petals are then reassembled to make up a rose. The only exceptions to this rule are the small single roses that are usually found only in a garden or in a tub on a patio, and rosebuds that can be sliced in half and hollowed out before pressing.

Exotic flowers were never a great success with the traditional flower-press, but now you can achieve perfect results on flowers like orchids, because the speed of the pressing stops them from turning brown. It is worth experimenting with any exotic varieties that may be available to you as they can give an unusual touch to your pressed flower repertoire.

The same standards of quality must apply to flowers from the florist as well; if a flower is damaged, brown or just past its best then, unless you have a specific reason for needing to press it, I would suggest rejecting it.

TABLE OF SUITABLE FLOWERS

NAME	COLOURS	PRESSING NOTES
Aconitum (Monkshood)	Dark blue/violet	Press individual flowers as well as small spikes of buds.
Agapanthus	Blue/white	Colour is not always kept reliably.
Ageratum	Blue/white	Press in small clusters.
Alchemilla (Lady's-mantle)	Yellow/green	Make sure flowers are well open or they may be lumpy.
Allium (ornamental onion)	Purple/white	Must be pressed in small pieces.
Alstroemeria (Peruvian lily)	Many	Press sideways and keep whole or they become transparent.
Amaryllis	Pink/red/white	Very large for pressing.
Ammobium	White	Can look crumpled and lumpy when pressed. May be better as a dried flower.
Anemone	Red/blue/white	Presses well. Remove as much black pollen as possible.
Anthemis	Yellow	Good colour retention.
Anthurium	Various	Difficult to press but possible.
Aquilegia (Columbine)	Various	Pick the smallest sizes.
Arachnis (Spider orchid)	Yellow/pink/ red spotted	Excellent colour retention.
Aster	Red/pink/blue	Solidaster – the yellow variety is excellent. Red aster also very good.
Astilbe	Pink/white red	Strong shape which can be difficult to use.
Astrantia	Pink/white	Presses well, but use smaller sizes.

NAME	COLOURS	PRESSING NOTES
Bellis (Daisy)	White/pink	Use only semi-double not pom-pom varieties as they are too thick.
Calendula (Marigold)	Yellow/orange	Good colour
Carnation	Many	Bi-coloured are particularly effective, but all press well.
Cattleya (Orchid)	Pink/lilac/ yellow/white	Takes time and care but presses beautifully.
Centaurea (Cornflower)	Blue/pink/ red/white	Excellent colour retention; needs extra weight on flowers.
Chamaelaucium (Wax flower)	White/pink	Press singly and in sprays.
Cheiranthus (Wallflower)	Shades of red/orange	Individual blooms press best.
Chrysanthemum	Many	Single varieties like marguerites are fine; the very heavy heads would have to be pressed petal by petal and then reconstructed.
Cineraria	Many including bi-coloured	Petals sometimes become detached and have to be glued back later.
Clarkia	Many	Semi-double are better than double as they look a little 'squashed' when pressed.
Clematis	White/pink/purple	Rare in florists but press well.
Convolvulus	Blue/pink/white	Fragile, but can look very pretty.
Coreopsis	Yellow	Centres can be troublesome to press.
Cosmos	Red/pink/white	Can become a little transparent; use small flowers
Crocosmia (Montbretia)	Orange/red	Buds curve nicely.
Cyclamen	Pink/white/red	Interesting shapes.
Cymbidium	Yellow/green/ white/salmon	Popular wedding flowers; pressed carefully, they work well.

NAME	COLOURS	PRESSING NOTES
Delphinium	Blue/purple	Presses beautifully; pink variety does not keep its colour – reverts to blue.
Delphinium (Larkspur)	Pink/white/blue	One of the most popular flowers for pressing; keeps colour really well and is very useful.
Dendrobium (Orchid)	Pink/white	Takes a few moments longer than some flowers but with good results.
Dicentra	White/pink	Unusual shape and good leaves.
Dill	White/yellow	Individual florets or whole heads can be useful.
Dimorphotheca	Orange/white	White presses well.
Euphorbia	Orange/red	Tiny flowers press better singly.
Forsythia	Yellow	Mediocre but can be used.
Freesia	Several	Red and blue colours change in pressing and darken. Press single flowers and sprays of buds and stems.
Fuchsia	Red/pink/purple	Smaller outdoor varieties press more successfully than the larger cultivated varieties.
Galanthus (Snowdrop)	White	Usually turns cream.
Genista (Broom)	White/yellow	Also available dyed in many colours.
Geranium	White/pink/red	Variable results; wild varieties press more successfully.
Gerbera	Many	The mini varieties are more useful.
Gypsophila	White	Very simple to press.
Heather	Pink/white	Wild variety presses best as some cultivated heathers are too lumpy.
Hebe	White/violet	Small sprays can be useful.

NAME	COLOURS	PRESSING NOTES
Helleborus (Christmas rose)	White/purple	Always presses well.
Heuchera	Pink/red	Easy to press; good colour.
Hyacinth	Pink/blue/white	Press single florets and then reconstruct.
Hydrangea	Blue/pink/white	Presses better in autumn when colour is retained.
Iberis (Candytuft)	Purple/pink/white	Sometimes shape is poor.
Iris	White/yellow/blue	Can be very good but unreliable.
Jasmine	White/yellow	Both leaves and flowers are useful.
Lavender	Blue	One of my favourites; it needs extra weight.
Lilies	Many	Most are successful; see tip in next section for stargazer lilies.
Lily-of-the-valley	White	Turns cream, but a good shape.
Lonicera (Honeysuckle)	White/yellow	Pretty shapes; press singly.
Lunaria (Honesty)	White/purple	Flowers excellent; seed pods also good when they are green and pearly white.
Mimosa	Yellow	Needs extra weight.
Muscari (Grape hyacinth)	Blue	Pretty shape; very slow to press.
Myosotis (Forget-me-not)	Blue/pink	Pink reverts magically to blue while inside the press!
Narcissus	Yellow/white	Soleil d'Or variety is excellent.
Nicotiana (Tobacco plant)	White/cream/ yellow	Press flowers on their side or full-face.
Nigella (Love-in-a-mist)	Blue/pink/white	Colour is a little weak but interesting shape when pressed.

NAME	COLOURS	PRESSING NOTES
Pansy	Various	So easy to press and such lovely faces!
Peony	Pink/red	Dismantle and press petals singly, then reconstruct.
Philadelphus (Mock orange)	White	Pretty yellow stamens.
Phlox	White/pink	Press single flowers; can be transparent.
Poppy	Various	Disappointing red – can become very fragile and transparent.
Potentilla	White/yellow/ red/orange	Very useful round flower which grows in great profusion.
Primula	Many	Red turns brown/black.
Rose	Many	All press well, including buds.
Statice	Many	Fiercely strong colour, can be difficult to press.
Stephanotis	White	Not easy to press; often bruises and turns cream or brown.
Sweet pea	Pink/blue	Very fragile flower with sporadic results when pressing; can be good.
Tulip	Various	Small tulips are more usable; parrot tulips retain fantastic colours.
Viburnum	White	Tiny flowers and buds useful for miniature work.
Vinca (Periwinkle)	Blue/white	Flowers can be pressed side or full-face.
Violet	White/violet	Presses well; try side and full-face.
Wisteria	White/mauve	Tedious pressing floret by floret and reconstructing, but very beautiful when you take the time!

HERBS, LEAVES AND MISCELLANEOUS

Nearly all leaves and herbs can be pressed successfully by the microwave method, the only drawback being that anything green will be the first thing in a design to fade when exposed to light. So it may be better to keep greens to a minimum in pictures or anything for which you have long-term plans.

I particularly recommend pressing variegated foliage by microwave. When using the traditional method, I found the cream and yellow portions of a variegated leaf often went brown. Not so with the microwave. Cream and green ivy and holly have been particularly successful and are now often included in our repertoire.

Shape and size should also be considered when choosing foliage to press. There are so many leaves that are absolutely enormous when pressed and tend to dwarf any flowers in the same design. Even hybrid tea roses tend to have leaves that are too large to use – I usually substitute a wild rose or species rose leaf. No one ever notices and it makes the flower look much more important.

You can also experiment with unusual things like chillies (be very careful and use rubber gloves to avoid burning yourself). Many vegetables and fungi will press successfully and may give you an idea for a project. So keep an open mind and experiment, consider a plant a success until it is proven otherwise, rather than writing it off before it has a chance to prove itself!

The table of flowers is just a beginning – you can also press many hundreds of different types of flowers, leaves, weeds and herbs that I have left unmentioned. Although herbs may not always be in flower, they can still be very useful in your designs. Likewise, don't forget foliage. Grey leaves are by far the prettiest as they keep their colour beautifully and contrast well with other elements in a picture. However microwave techniques retain greens well and they obviously go with everything and so have many uses.

If you are not sure whether something will press or not then try it – nothing ventured, nothing gained!

$\mathcal{B}$asic Pressing Techniques

For those who have never attempted any pressing before, I feel it is useful to include here a short section on traditional pressing techniques. Although microwave pressing is quicker and more exciting, the traditional way of pressing is less labour-intensive and sometimes produces equally good results. When large quantities of pressed flowers and leaves are needed, as they are constantly for our pressed flower picture business, we have neither the time nor the personnel to press everything by means of the microwave. At some times of the year, for example, we need to press tens of thousands of larkspur flowers; these have to be processed in the old-fashioned way just to cope with the huge volume each day.

So, although I hope you will find the new ideas of tremendous use, there will always be times when the old-fashioned (and very portable) flower press will still be needed.

TRADITIONAL FLOWER PRESSING

A standard flower press is made from two pieces of plywood about 1 cm (½ in) thick. These should have holes drilled in each corner and four bolts and screws inserted in the holes. You then need blotting paper and newspaper to fill the press. I usually suggest eleven wads of newspaper (about the normal thickness of a daily paper) and twenty pieces of blotting paper, cut to size. These should be a little bit smaller than the press so that they all fit neatly inside. The usual size that we make our presses is about 20 cm × 20 cm (8 × 8 in) but you can buy presses from craft shops or similar outlets in many sizes.

YOU WILL NEED

2 pieces of 20 cm (8 in) square
plywood

4 bolts, 7.5 cm (3 in) long

4 wing nuts to fit the bolts

4 washers

11 pads of newspaper
(each approximately 10 sheets thick),
cut to fit the press

20 sheets of blotting paper, cut to fit
the press

Place the two pieces of plywood on top of each other, ensuring that they are completely square, and tape or clamp them together. Drill a hole in each of the four corners, about 1 cm (½ in) from each side, using a drill bit that is slightly larger than the diameter of the four bolts that you intend to use. Don't choose bolts that are much longer than 7.5 cm (3 in), as the press will be unwieldy and difficult to store or carry about. Finally, you will need the four wing nuts and washers to hold the bolts firm as you tighten the press.

USING A FLOWER PRESS

Once you have made or acquired your press, check that you have enough newspaper and blotting paper. If you have bought the press, you may find that it contains corrugated card in the press. This tends to leave unsightly stripes across anything that you press, and should be consigned to the bin and replaced with newspaper. Cut the blotting paper and newspaper to the correct size to fit inside the press without touching the bolts.

You can now use your press. Flowers should be picked the first day that they bloom. See instructions for selecting and picking on page 11. Place a layer of newspaper in the bottom of the press, and cover it with a piece of blotting paper. Then lay your first few flowers on to the blotting paper. Make sure that the backs and fronts of the flowers have been well trimmed, so that they are as flat as possible. Never pick flowers when they are wet from rain or excessive dew; try to wait an hour or two if it is a very misty or dewy morning as this gives the flowers time to dry out before pressing.

Never overlap the flowers in the press or they will leave marks on the other flowers, and do not place them too near the edge of the press or they may escape the overall pressure and wrinkle up. When the first layer is complete, cover with a sheet of blotting paper, then a wad of newspaper and begin with another piece of blotting paper. It is a little like making sandwiches, if you imagine the newspaper is the bread, the blotting paper the butter and the flowers the filling in the middle! I usually fill the press with approximately ten layers (flowers, newspapers and blotting paper).

If you are pressing anything very thick or lumpy with very thin or delicate flowers, I would suggest using different presses. It is best to keep the layers as even as possible so that all the material receives an even pressure. When pressing thicker material, use only two or three layers in the press.

Once you have filled the press, place the second piece of wood on top and tighten the screws until you cannot make them any tighter. Label the press with a piece of masking tape (so that it is easily removable later) with the date that you have filled it press, what's inside and perhaps where you picked the flowers, for later reference. Then put it in a warm place (such as an airing cupboard) for at least six weeks.

Your flowers will then be ready to use. They can be left in the press for much longer if it is inconvenient to empty it then. Alternatively, the contents can be filed away in clear-fronted cellophane bags and kept in a warm dry place, preferably sealed in a fairly airtight container.

Although you are a little more limited in what will press and what will not, this method has been around for many years. If you don't own a microwave you could still make many of the projects in the book, with perhaps a slight adjustment of certain ingredients.

PRESSING WITH BOOKS

It is not essential to buy or make a flower press as adequate results can be obtained by using telephone directories or heavy books. Some flowers and leaves even seem to prefer being pressed in books rather than being subjected to the constant extreme pressure of a flower press. Choose a book with absorbent pages rather than a glossy encyclopedia. Make blotting paper folders slightly larger than the telephone directory or old book that you are using. Slot about five blotting paper folders into the book at equal intervals. As a general rule of thumb, the lighter and flimsier the flower, the less pressure it takes to press successfully. So a single rose petal may press extremely successfully in a book, while a heavier flower like a gerbera will need the extra weight of a press.

Prepare your flowers for pressing as before and place them into the first folder. Keep them away from the edges so that enough pressure is applied to achieve an even finish. Continue to fill the other folders. Label the book with dates, contents and places, and place it under two or three heavy books (now the encyclopedias come into their own!) and leave for six weeks.

Do make sure that you store your presses or books in a warm dry place. Often people use garages or outbuildings; these are not warm enough, as the temperature will fall during the night. If you live in a very humid climate, try to keep the presses warm and away from humidity. It may help to seal them in polythene bags. If humidity is a problem, I would recommend that you rely more heavily on the microwave method.

CHAPTER 3

Microwave Pressing

Now that you have some knowledge of older techniques, you will discover how quick and easy this new method is in comparison. The first and most important thing to realize is that all microwave ovens seem to react in roughly the same fashion, with slight differences. So all the instructions I give are based on a 600-watt oven and must be varied to suit yours. Having said that, one of the microwaves we use regularly is a 400-watt antique version with only on, defrost and off switches, as opposed to the sophisticated computerised versions now available now, and it uses almost identical timings.

The best time and temperature to begin with is two minutes on a medium heat. This is a good starting point for most flowers and leaves and should not cause any burning problems but should see most flowers well on their way to drying. But first to equipment ...

MAKING A MICROWAVE PRESS

YOU WILL NEED
2 pieces of hardboard approximately
25 x 20 cm (10 x 8 in)
(or a suitable size to fit inside your
microwave and turn without catching)
5 or 6 thick elastic bands, approximately
5 mm (¼ in) wide
6 pieces of blotting paper, cut to
24 x 19 cm (9½ x 7½ in)

These ingredients will make up one microwave press. However, I would suggest that you have at least six of these ready to use in rotation, as they take a little time to cool down.

You will also need extra elastic bands as they break with use; the hot temperatures weaken them and they occasionally pop while in the oven. One way around this is to make some elastic straps from lengths of dress elastic. Just measure the elastic carefully and tie it in a non-slip knot, so that it holds the press together securely but does not stretch the elastic to its limits.

Extra blotting paper is also advisable as there are occasions when a particularly wet item may damage the blotting paper or the paper may just wear thin with constant use.

USING A MICROWAVE PRESS

Lay one piece of hardboard (rough side inside) on a table and cover it with three pieces of blotting paper. Place your flowers or leaves on top. Do not overfill the press; it is always better to press too few items rather than too many at a time. You will only be cooking one layer at a time. Keep all the flowers well within the confines of the paper and don't allow any of them to overlap. Then cover them with the other three sheets of blotting paper, and place the second piece of hardboard on top.

Now hold the whole sandwich together with the elastic bands. Place three across each side of the press so that they cross each other and hold the press firmly shut. This is essential as it creates the pressure that ensures the flowers are completely flat when they emerge from the press later.

If you are pressing something lumpy, like lavender or a flower with a thick centre, I have found this is a good time to flatten it with a little extra weight. Place the press on the floor and carefully stand on it (about 64 kilos/10 st works perfectly, but if you weigh more or less, don't panic!) This process can be repeated for particularly resilient contents after the two minutes in the microwave.

Now that you have loaded the press, place it in the microwave. Set the temperature to medium and cook for two minutes. When ready, do not be tempted to open the press and look inside. Place the warm (sometimes quite hot) package under several telephone directories to weigh it down and leave it until it has completely cooled. Hence my suggestion that you have several presses on the go at once so that you can immediately load another press and circulate them until you can reuse your original press.

Once the press is cool (which usually takes at least twenty minutes), carefully open it and, using tweezers, very gently touch or move the flowers to check whether they are completely dry. It is no use having something 'almost dry' as it will discolour as it dries in the final stages. Make sure that it is completely dry and not limp. If there are any signs of dampness, wrap it up again and put it back in the oven for another two minutes. Leave to cool and then check again.

STEP 1

Make any necessary preparations to your flowers. Here, the roses have to be stripped and the petals pressed singly.

STEP 2

Assemble your microwave press following the instructions. Make sure you have all the ingredients.

STEP 3

Cover a piece of hardboard with half the blotting paper. Place the petals on the paper, cover with the remaining sheets and place another piece of hardboard on top. Secure with the elastic bands.

STEP 4

Cook on medium power for two minutes. Remove the press from the oven and leave to cool under a couple of heavy books.

STEP 5

Check the contents of the press to see if they are dry. If not, repeat the process and check again.

STEP 6

Once the petals are dry, leave overnight under some books and then remove from the blotting paper. It is important to keep them out of the light, so store in paper bags in an airtight container.

This process should dry many simple flowers and leaves. However, there are major exceptions, of which orchids are one. Orchids are very fleshy flowers and take much longer to dry. I usually start them with five minutes on medium heat and then check again when they are cool, perhaps cooking in two-minute bursts after that. This means that the process takes a little longer, but the slow and steady approach tends to be more successful. If you get carried away and give too much heat for too long, then at best you will get blistering and disfigurement of the flower or leaf, or it will be completely burnt and all your hard work will be ruined.

Take the greatest care not to use your microwave oven on full power as you run a grave risk of burning the hardboard. This discolours the oven, leaves a layer of black greasy soot all over the inside and ruins two perfectly good pieces of hardboard and the blotting paper. However, it is inevitable that this will happen at some point. It has happened to me several times over the last few years. It is so easy to get carried away with your enthusiasm and the frustration that the process is not happening in seconds rather than minutes. We flower pressers are such impatient souls. So be warned – take things slowly and methodically and all will be well.

Once you are satisfied that the flowers or leaves are well dried, leave them between the pieces of blotting paper in a pile near a radiator. Place three or four telephone directories on top and leave them overnight. This helps to make sure that they are properly dry and cool before you use them. You can then check them the next morning.

If you simply have to use your pressed bits and pieces on the same day that you pick them, do make absolutely sure that they are dry and completely cool. If a flower is not quite cool, it can mask any dampness left inside.

STORAGE

Once flowers or leaves are completely dry, it is important to keep them in a dry atmosphere, away from humidity and air generally and out of the light. The best way is to keep them in sealed bags in an airtight container. For extra caution in humid periods, or if you live in a country that suffers a great deal of humidity, you could keep a few silica gel crystals in the box where you store your flowers and regularly re-dry them.

KEEPING MICROWAVE RECORDS

This is the point at which you must start keeping records of your microwave pressing. If you note down now any times or notes that you can, then when you next want to press that particular flower you will know how long it took in your oven. So a note might read: 'Red rose petals – took 2 minutes – needed no extra treatment.' For lavender it might say: 'Hidcote blue lavender – extra pressure after first cooking then needed two more sessions to dry.' (These are not exact records, just examples.)

I have also found that the same flower can require varying times, depending upon the amount of moisture in a particular batch. If you are buying from a florist rather than picking from the garden, I often find the time varies from bunch to bunch, depending on how long the flowers have been in water and how recently the florist has bought them. If you stick to the basic two minutes, then cool and check, you should have very few problems.

The problems start when you try to speed up the process. Cooking a flower for four minutes solidly does not have the same effect as cooking for two minutes, cooling, then cooking for another two minutes. The four-minute spell in the oven will produce more heat and may even burn the flower. Having said that, if you have a particularly moisture-filled bunch of specimens to dry, you may want to increase the initial cooking time after a little experimentation. An orchid rarely takes less than seven minutes but I would still cook it for about four minutes and then cool, and cook again for two or more minutes, as I am always nervous of burning the flowers.

On pages 98–109 of this book you will find that I have provided you with some charts to start you off on keeping microwave records.

EXTRA PREPARATION TIPS

Several flowers need extra care and time spent on them before pressing and I hope these tips will save you some of the time and patience that I have had to expend in experimenting with this technique.

Try to look objectively at all the specimens you pick and imagine them flattened. Some may look better pressed on their side, some full-face. In many cases I experiment with both and then pick the most successful versions later when I am using them. Some centres may need to be completely removed and pressed separately or not at all. If this is the case, you can substitute a false centre later on. Hellebores, for example, need to have their centres removed as they do not seem to press very successfully otherwise. You can then either press the centre on its own, or use a floret from a piece of cow parsley or the centre from a daisy or potentilla as a false centre later.

POLLEN

There are several flowers with troublesome pollen. One is the anemone, which presses absolutely beautifully, but the black pollen can be a tedious nuisance when you get to picture or project stage. Before you microwave the flowers, gently tap them to remove as much excess pollen as possible, then, using a small brush, remove a little more pollen. Finally, spray them with a little hair spray to fix the pollen and help to hold it in position.

The lily is another problem flower. Its orange pollen is a major disaster area. I find the easiest way to deal with it is to trim the tops off the stamens and throw them away. However, if you are determined that you want the stamens complete with pollen, try to remove as much as possible before pressing. The pollen will stain and spoil any blotting paper with which it comes into contact, so you have been warned!

Any other problem pollen areas can probably be dealt with in the same way as the anemone – dust off as much as possible and then fix with hair spray.

ROSEBUDS

Rosebuds look fabulous pressed with this technique but need a little extra care in preparation. Slice the rosebud into two pieces if it is fairly small. If it is larger, three or four slices might be easier, but discard the middle pieces and use only the outside slices that have some coloured petals and green sepals covering them.

These outer segments should carry on down into the stem so that you have about 1.5 cm (⅝ in) of stem and a small piece of rosebud attached. Handle each very carefully as they are very delicate and fragile at this stage. Turn the bud over and remove any curled-up pieces of petal that are tightly balled at the base of the bud. The only petals remaining should be the few that show at the top of the bud. Take care not to remove too much and end up with the rosebud in shreds.

Then place the bud slices on the sheet of blotting paper and proceed as before. If you have a slightly large rosebud half, a little extra weight might be necessary, but take care; if you stand on a large rosebud half with careless abandon, you may find that when you open the press, the rosebud looks bruised and squashed. Try pressing hard with your hand and leaning on it; this will add extra weight without destroying the bud.

STEMS

Many of the projects in this book have used stems of one variety or another. I always press a few spare stems when I have time as they are often needed for posy pictures, and it is useful to have them to hand. Some stems, such as roses, are too woody to press, but others, such as anemones, are easy to press with a little preparation.

Split your stem in half and then scoop out any fibres inside to make it as easy to press as possible. If the fibres are hard to remove, try using a pan scrubber or the blade of a blunt knife. Then press the stem with plenty of extra weight (stand on the press after one cooking) if necessary.

TIPS ON IMPROVING YOUR END RESULTS

When I last visited Japan I was given an excellent tip by one of Japan's most brilliant flower pressers and artists, Nobuo Sugino. His school has many different ways to preserve flowers but this one was a particularly effective tip and I thank him for allowing me to include it in my book.

The red area on the petals of stargazer lilies tends to deaden when pressed and this process brightens them noticeably.

BRIGHTENING STARGAZER LILIES

STEP 1

Pour a little white wine vinegar into a small bowl. Either apply directly to the petals using an artist's brush, or soak a piece of blotting paper in the vinegar and press it over the petals. Then cover them with a fresh sheet of blotting paper.

STEP 3

Check the finished result and, if necessary, repeat the whole process: both the vinegar and the pressing – it may brighten them slightly more. But do not overdo this. Make sure that the petals are completely dry before using.

STEP 2

Using an iron set to medium temperature, press it over the petals for the count of ten.

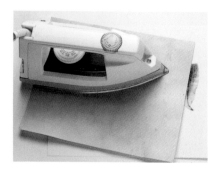

In principle, I am against enhancing the colour of flowers in pressed flower work, as I like the natural colours that can be achieved using this pressing method. However, there have been occasions when I have made something and varnished it and from choice displayed it in bright sunshine. I had a hat box on my bedroom window-sill for a whole summer. I enjoyed looking at it but by the autumn the flowers were completely faded; I loved the box and, being unwilling to replace it, I experimented with replacing the colour lost from the flowers.

Having tried every paint known to mankind – or, to be more exact, every paint known to the very helpful man at my local hardware store – I came across a paint used specifically for glass painting. I tried several colours of this paint and hey presto! The fact that the flowers had been varnished meant that they were resistant to ordinary emulsion and many varieties of paint that I tried looked heavy and immediately unrealistic. The glass paint, however, looks very natural and works quickly and instantly. It can also be diluted if necessary with spirit. You still have to be very gentle with your 'touching up' and use the colour subtly or it can look garish and ghastly.

The amount of time it takes to pretty up something that has faded is still unrealistic for anything commercial, but for a one-off project or two at home this is a very useful additional technique.

COMMON PROBLEMS

Certain situations can arise when a little first aid may be necessary for your stocks of flowers. Sometimes small insects can be picked with the flowers, hatching out after pressing. This is pretty unlikely in microwave-pressed flowers but can be a nuisance when flowers are pressed traditionally. The best way to solve this problem is to place the cellophane bag complete with flowers and any offending 'creepy crawlies' in the microwave and cook it for two minutes on medium heat. You may need to apply some light pressure afterwards to make sure the flowers do not curl up.

Plagues of tiny creeping things can also be the result of using old blotting paper that has become infested with these bugs. Again, a few spells in a microwave usually removes the problem. Reusing cellophane bags may also cause infestations, as these bags can provide a suitable place for insects – or more correctly insects' eggs – to lurk. It is very tempting to use the bags over and over again for storing flowers in; although I do not advocate using them only once, a few months or at most a season is probably sufficient.

There will also be many times when you come to use a flower and find a damaged or disfigured petal. In a picture, it may be possible to hide this under another flower. Alternatively, you can replace a damaged petal with one from another flower and carefully glue it to the centre.

CHAPTER 2

Simply Beautiful

All the designs featured in this section are very simple and can be copied by anyone with a basic knowledge of pressed flowers and a little patience. The projects are fairly speedy to make as the flowers are left uncovered. They are, nevertheless, fairly secure as quite a bit of glue is used to make sure that they are well stuck on to the surface being decorated. Cards and paper projects tend to have a shorter life than more complex designs, so leaving the flowers unprotected is rarely a problem.

However, if you want to make absolutely sure that your design is going to remain in the same place and stay in pristine condition, you can cover it with laminating film. This is available from some stationers as it is sometimes used to cover books, or mail-order (see page 110). There are several varieties, ranging from glossy and semi-glossy to matt finishes. I prefer the matt finish as I feel it does not detract so much from the flowers. The glossy finish can initially attract the eye away from the flower design.

If it is not absolutely necessary to cover them, I love pressed flowers plain, with no covering at all, as you can see so much detail. However, if you are not covering the flowers and leaves, it is essential that you glue down every tiny piece of the design. The best way to achieve this is first to place a circular puddle of white latex adhesive on an old dinner plate or piece of glass. Then, holding the flower or leaf with your tweezers, brush it over the pool of glue, making sure that it completely covered. Gently brush the flower or leaf against the side of the plate to remove any excess glue, then place it into the design. As the glue dries up you can remove it by rubbing it with a piece of kitchen towel and then with your fingers. Being rubber-based, it will roll into a ball and is easily removable. Then start with a new puddle of glue.

With all these projects, as well as those featured later in the book, it is always a good idea to press many more flowers, leaves or stems than you imagine you might need. This allows for mishaps in the pressing process, but, if you have picked plenty, you needn't make a drama out of a crisis! It is also always amazing how many leaves and flowers you can use in what seems like a pretty moderately-sized project. So, collect more than you think necessary and the leftovers will always come in handy for another idea later on.

Obviously, all these projects are shown with specific flowers or leaves, but do not be deterred by the fact that you may not have access to a particular flower or bush. Look at the basic idea of the project and change it to fit the flowers and leaves you can access easily; you may well come up with an even better combination.

Lavender Sweet Lavender

Greetings cards can convey many different messages, but the overall intention is to send someone a special thought. People will treasure a handmade card as much as, if not more than, a present. If it is for a special occasion you will want to make it with a particular recipient in mind. But for general birthday or celebration cards, why not spend a few evenings microwaving some flowers and turning them into a stock of greetings cards, at very little cost.

YOU WILL NEED

Scissors

Sheet of handmade paper in the desired shade

Tweezers

Pressed lavender flowers with long stems

Lavender leaves

White latex adhesive

Old dinner plate or piece of glass

Sheet of medium-weight card

Double-sided tape

STEP 1

Cut the handmade paper to a slightly smaller size than you want the finished card to be. Using the tweezers, arrange the lavender stems and leaves on the paper, gluing as you go. Alternatively, arrange them first, then glue them in place afterwards, but this takes a lot longer.

STEP 2

Make the clump of lavender look full, as though it was part of a healthy bush rather than a spindly bunch. Refer to the beginning of this chapter for gluing techniques. Take care that the glue is not too visible; if you use too much, it will ooze out from behind the flowers and leaves and look very unsightly.

STEP 3

Once your design is complete, leave it for a short while to allow the glue to dry. If you go and make a cup of coffee, or just leave it overnight, when you come back to the design you may well see it differently and spot something that needs adding or changing.

STEP 4

Cut a folded piece of card to size (larger than the paper). Fix the lavender-decorated paper centrally on the folded card with double-sided tape. You could also sign your work or add the botanical name of the lavender. Use a fine pen or a subtle colour of ink, or the writing might dominate the design.

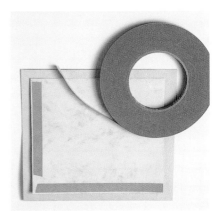

How About?

Group ordinary lawn daisies on a dark coloured paper. They keep their colour beautifully, and pink-edged ones look wonderful. Press some of them on their sides to give different shapes to work with.

Sweet Herbs and Savory

This design uses parsley leaves, but most herbs will be just as effective. A bunch of flowering thyme or rosemary looks very pretty, while mint with its flowers makes a lovely display. There are many different varieties of herb available fresh or growing in pots; you could experiment with all of them. Several terracotta pots could be grouped on one card with different herbs or flowers growing in them.

YOU WILL NEED

Scissors

Sheet of handmade paper in a terracotta shade

Sheet of stiff card

Sheet of handmade paper in a lighter colour

White latex adhesive

Tweezers

Pressed parsley

Old dinner plate or piece of glass

Double-sided tape

STEP 1

Cut a flowerpot shape out of the terracotta-coloured paper. Decide on your finished card size and cut both the stiff card and the handmade paper to stick on to it. The paper should be a little smaller than the finished card size, to give a border effect.

STEP 2

Glue the flowerpot shape on to the handmade paper in a suitable position. Leave to dry for a little while.

STEP 3

Carefully glue the parsley in position, using the all-over gluing technique (see page 35). Try to ensure that some of the pieces hang over the edge of the pot to make it more realistic. Press each piece down gently and then leave to dry.

STEP 4

Attach some double-sided tape to the underside of the piece of paper, along all four edges, and stick the paper on to the card. You can sign the card or add the name of the herb. Another possibility is to enclose a few details of the herb, or perhaps a packet of seeds or a recipe inside the card. A thoughtful gift might be one of your favourite herbal recipes, with the pressed herbs on the front of the card, the recipe and a packet of seeds inside.

How About?

Another idea for using pressed herbs is to write out a beauty recipe, like mint foot bath or rose hand cream, on the front of the card and to border it with the relevant flowers or herbs. There are many books on homemade lotions and potions to give you ideas for recipes.

A Rose by any other Name?

These cards all use various species roses, particularly single varieties. There are many different kinds of patio rose and species rose that press brilliantly (see lists of possible plants to press starting on page 14). Here they have been used to give a botanical feel to the cards. Rose leaves vary in size and colour throughout the year as well and these might add to the interest of your design. Use small ones in appropriate places.

YOU WILL NEED

Assorted pieces of card
Scissors
White latex adhesive
Old dinner plate or piece of glass
Tweezers
Pressed roses and foliage

All these examples have been made using the all-over gluing method (see page 35) and contain various roses with their leaves and buds. Rose leaves are better pressed in the early part of the season before they become too large. Alternatively, you can use some smaller varieties.

STEP 1

It is often easier to begin your card design by choosing an envelope. It is possible to make your own, but the quickest and easiest way is to buy a pack of good-quality envelopes from a local stationers. Once you have the size of your envelope, you can then cut your card to a suitable size to fit into it. Or you could use some of the many different blank cards available from craft shops and by mail-order (see useful addresses on page 110).

STEP 2

Arrange pressed roses and leaves on the card, holding them with tweezers. There is no need to use too many flowers on a greetings card, as the card will be inspected at very close range and it is nice to have just a few really beautiful preserved flowers, rather than covering the whole card with flowers and taking away from the individual beauty of each bloom. Glue them in place using the all-over gluing method.

STEP 3

Gift tags are very quick and easy to make and are an excellent way of using up the smaller scraps of card or paper that tend to accumulate once you begin making your own cards. Make tags in the same way as you would cards, but smaller. Thread a small piece of pretty ribbon or cord through the corner to add a finishing touch.

How About?

Try making a botanical-style card showing the rose plant at various stages. The buds press well, providing that you cut them in half to make them a little thinner. The rose hips could also be used by reducing the bulk in a similar manner. Choose small rosehips to start with and then cut them down to make them as thin as possible before pressing them.

Decorated Drawer Liners

Whether it is a drawer that you use frequently, or just a small chest in a guest room, these drawer liners will add a special floral touch. They are also scented with essential oil to add a natural fragrance to the room and the contents of the drawer. They are very simple to make.

YOU WILL NEED

Scissors

Large pieces of paper (I used a paper made with flowers and petals)

Small bottle of essential oil of your choice

Clingfilm

Tweezers

Pressed flowers and leaves

White latex adhesive

Old dinner plate or piece of glass

Optional heat-seal film

STEP 1

Cut the pieces of paper to fit the drawers that you wish to line. Once they fit well in the drawer, remove them and sprinkle with a few drops of essential oil. Then roll the paper and wrap securely in clingfilm, sealing the ends. Store for about a week to allow the essential oil to perfume the entire piece of paper.

STEP 2

Once the paper is ready, flatten it by rolling it in the opposite direction. Then, using tweezers, scatter the flowers on to the paper in the design of your choice. Glue them down carefully using the all-over gluing method (see page 35).

STEP 3

If you intend to use the drawer extensively, or wish to be able to wipe the drawer lining, it would be better to cover the entire piece of paper with some heat-seal film or laminating film. Alternatively, you can decorate the paper in patches and just cover those patches with film. This film is available by mail-order and comes complete with instructions. To use it, you just peel off the backing paper and place the film over the flowers. Then press with a moderate iron to laminate the film to the paper.

How About?

Try matching the essential oil to the pressed items that are used for the liner. Roses could be paired with rose oil, and tiny slivers of orange and lemon peel could be paired with a citrus oil. Jasmine leaves and flowers press well, but the flowers would have to be placed against a darker coloured paper. They could then be scented with jasmine oil. There are as many combinations as there are oils.

Pressed for (Tea) Time!

This is a lovely idea that makes a small present even more interesting. Herbal tea bags can be bought individually and then if you package them in a decorated envelope, they become too pretty to use. You could also use standard tea bags and decorate with specially chosen garden flowers.

YOU WILL NEED

Scissors

Medium- to heavy-weight handmade paper

Double-sided tape

Pressed herbs (I used fennel, mint and elderflower)

Tweezers

White latex adhesive

Old dinner plate or piece of glass

Pen

Herbal tea bags in flavours to match

Hole-punch (optional)

Ribbon or cord (optional)

STEP 1

Cut a piece of medium- to heavy-weight handmade paper into a long rectangle measuring approximately 30 × 12 cm (12 × 4¾ in). Place some double-sided tape along half of the two longer sides. Fold the rectangle in half, pressing down gently on the tape. This makes the basic bag.

STEP 2

Decorate each bag with a suitable herb to match the herbal tea bag that you are going to place inside. Use the all-over gluing method (see page 35). Take particular care not to put too much glue on fine, delicate-leaved herbs like fennel, or it will ooze through.

STEP 3

Press the flowers and leaves down and leave for a short while for the glue to dry.

STEP 4

Write the Latin name of the flower or herb and the brewing instructions for the tea on the back of the packet. You could also include some details of the ailments the tea will improve. Pop the tea bags in the bag. If you want to seal the bag, thread a small piece of ribbon or cord through a hole punched at the top.

How About?

You could try making the examples shown here, using elderflower, mint and fennel. There are many other herb and flower teas that you could match up, such as rose hip, hibiscus or camomile. If you are giving several sachets of the same variety of tea bag, they could be bundled together with a pretty ribbon. Scented pot pourri sachets could also be packaged in a similar way. Lavender sachets could be decorated with lavender, or a mixed garden pot pourri decorated with flowers like those in the mix.

ℳarriage Memories

Flowers are always a very important part of any marriage ceremony but not everybody wishes to preserve them afterwards in a very formal way (see wedding bouquet picture on pages 86/87). This wedding album keeps the pressed flowers in peak condition and gives a pretty and original reminder of the celebrations and of a very special day.

YOU WILL NEED

Pressed wedding flowers
Wedding album, with tissue paper between the pages
White latex adhesive
Old dinner plate or piece of glass
Tweezers
Scraps of confetti (optional)

STEP 1

Assemble all the lovingly-preserved flowers from the wedding, then separate them into suitable groups, such as small posies made from the corsage flowers, and a bunch composed of the church or reception flowers.

STEP 2

Using the all-over gluing method (see page 35), carefully compose groups of flowers on some of the pages. Take care not to overfill the album; there should be plenty of spaces for photographs.

STEP 3

Alternatively, you could plan the flowers around the wedding photographs, first mounting the photographs in the album, then arranging the flowers to correspond with the pictures. For example, as the couple are leaving in the wedding car, match some of the flowers in the photograph with the pressed flowers. You could also scatter a few pieces of confetti to decorate the pages; do not use too much glue, however, as they can go soggy.

How About?

Although this project was designed for wedding flowers, there are many other variations that would make wonderful souvenirs or special memories. How about a photograph album with flowers and pictures from your holiday? Or an album devoted to a house you have recently left and decorated with flowers pressed from the garden. The same principle could be applied to a christening ceremony, a silver wedding party or any other memorable occasion.

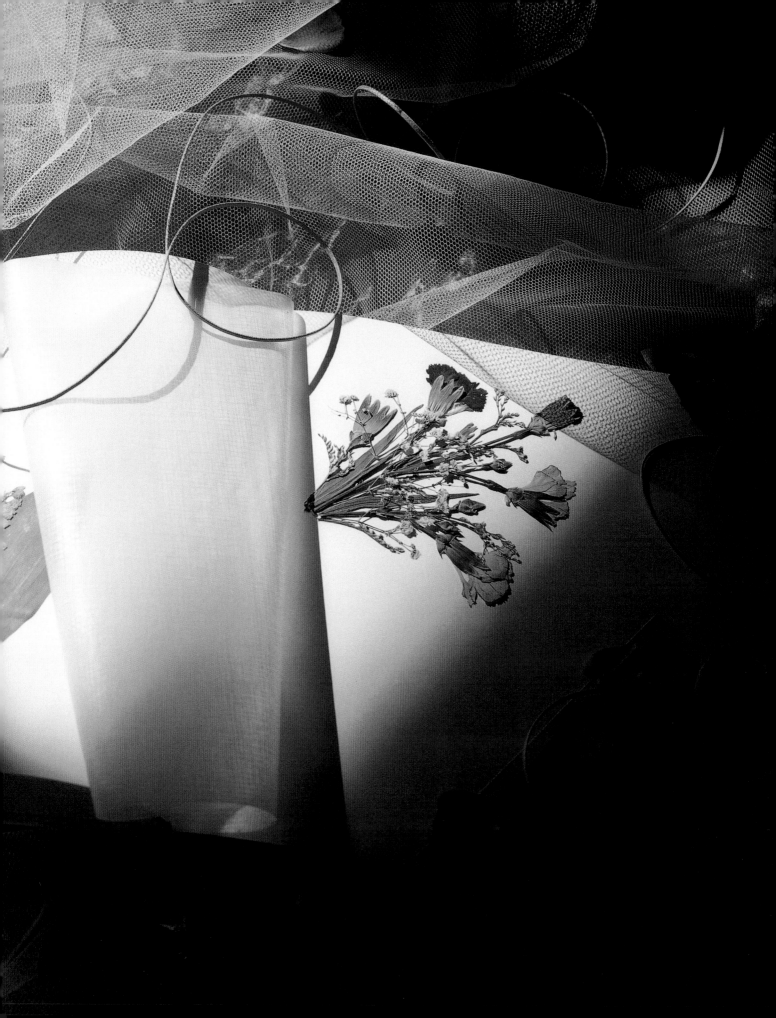

Floral Lampshade

Plain lampshades lend themselves well to anything from the most beautiful decorating techniques to something sweet and simple, like this sprigged effect with tiny pieces of forget-me-not. Flowers can be chosen for their colours or shapes or you could try a multi-coloured garden assortment to remind you of summer during long winter evenings.

YOU WILL NEED

White latex adhesive
Old dinner plate or piece of glass
Pieces of pressed forget-me-not with stalks and leaves
Tweezers
Plain lampshade
Laminating film or polyurethane varnish (optional)

STEP 1

Using the all-over gluing method (see page 35), stick the pieces of forget-me-not very firmly to the shade. You have to use the glue with care; although you need enough to anchor the flowers completely, you must avoid using too much and making a gluey mess of the shade.

STEP 2

Once the glue has dried, check the lampshade and gently remove any excess glue by rubbing it lightly with your finger or fingernail. The reason for this is that excess glue shows twice as much once the light is switched on. You should still aim to keep the lampshade out of strong sunlight, as you would a pressed flower picture.

STEP 3

If you want a more permanent decoration, you can cover the forget-me-nots with either laminating film or a coat of clear polyurethane varnish. Both methods work, but I find the uncovered version more attractive. If it needs replacing after some time, it takes very little effort to prise off the old flowers and replace them with new ones.

How About?

You could try stencilling a container on to the lampshade and 'filling' it with pressed flowers. I have experimented with stencilled wheelbarrows filled with pressed summer bedding plants. Another success was a stencilled blue and white container, to match the lamp base shown in the photograph, painted on to the shade and then 'filled' with blue and white flowers.

CHAPTER 5

Covered Flowers

Once the flower pressing bug grabs you, your mind wanders to what you can do with pressed flowers. Cards and stationery are always a good starting point and pressed flower pictures under glass will always be popular. But having experimented with both those types of projects for many years, I really wanted to find more ways of using my flower collection and different ways to display the results, without having to use up more wall space.

This coincided with a developing enthusiasm for traditional découpage, a craft which I have used very successfully to decorate all sorts of pieces of furniture and ornaments in the house. One day, while cutting out a particularly beautiful little rose from a piece of wrapping paper, I thought how much quicker it would be to use pressed flowers that do not need any cutting out. Immediately I rushed into dozens of projects in my enthusiasm to try out my new idea. Some worked well; others were disappointing.

I learned very quickly that you must seal all your flowers before you use them on any project that will be varnished. Often I found that once the varnish was applied, the flower became transparent, like a piece of onion skin. This is easily remedied by spraying with a floral sealant, available from garden centres and craft shops. They are sold to spray over dried flower arrangements but they are very useful with pressed flower projects as well.

You can either spray the flowers before they are attached to the item you are decorating or once they have been stuck in place and before the first coat of varnish is applied. I think it is marginally easier to spray them once they are in position, but if this is not convenient or possible, spraying before use is fine. Take care that the flowers do not curl up; if you are spraying loose flowers, wait for them to dry and then put them back between sheets of blotting paper and a light weight to make sure they do not spoil.

The key to success in traditional or pressed flower découpage is many, many layers of varnish. If you want a smooth mirror-like finish, you need to apply at least 20 coats of varnish, sanding after the first ten or so with very fine sandpaper. Take the greatest care doing this as it is so easy to spoil the flowers. The point of sanding is only to even out the varnish if there is a build-up or drip in one spot. However, depending on what you are decorating and whether it will be heavily used or not, you can get by with only half a dozen coats of varnish, but don't expect the same flawless finish. If you are decorating furniture, do make sure that there are enough layers of varnish to withstand the handling that it is likely to receive.

The best thing about using this technique is the wide variety of objects that you can decorate. Basically, if it is flat and will take varnish, then give it a go.

Recipe for Success

These plain papier mâché boxes can be bought from many craft shops and gift outlets. They make a very useful card index container but would also make an excellent present for a keen cook. You could use pressed herbs or something brighter like the brilliant scarlet chillies featured here.

YOU WILL NEED

Cloth
Blank papier mâché box
Pressed herbs or flowers
Tweezers
White latex adhesive
Old dinner plate or piece of glass
Floral sealant
Clear polyurethane varnish
Small brush
Set of index cards and dividers

STEP 1

Using a damp cloth, clean the outside of the box thoroughly to remove any dust or grease. Take care not to wet the papier mâché too much. Place your pressed herbs or flowers in position and glue down well. If you are using something like these bright red chillies, make sure that the whole length of the chilli is firmly attached to the box.

STEP 2

Once all your plant material is firmly attached to the box, gently spray with a coat of floral sealant.

STEP 3

When that has dried, paint over a coat of clear varnish. I use a quick-drying polyurethane varnish and like to apply at least eight or nine coats, especially over something a little lumpy like the chillies. You could possibly use only three or four coats over some flatter herbs.

STEP 4

Decorate some or all of the index cards to add extra colour and interest to the project. In this case I have included sage leaves, parsley, tarragon, flowering thyme and, of course, the chillies.

How About?

You could also decorate a similar box with more floral ingredients and use it as an address file; a mixture of roses and pansies with a little greenery would look lovely. You could make a personalized gift by writing, tracing or stencilling the recipient's name on to the centre of the box, then making a garland of pressed flowers around it.

A Blanket of Roses

This large blanket box could just as easily have been a toy box or a general purpose box. This example was made from new pine, but you could also use an old box that you might find in a junk shop or a trunk that has been tucked away in the attic. You could always mix paper cut-outs and pressed flowers to help cover the large spaces on a project this size. Alternatively, you could also stencil a design of pots or urns on the box, then 'fill' them with pressed flowers.

YOU WILL NEED

Cloth

Large box, in plain unfinished wood

Car spray paint in red and mossy green

Large pressed flowers and leaves
(I used Robin Redbreast roses
and leaves and some *Alchemilla mollis* flowers)

Paper

Tweezers

White latex adhesive

Old dinner plate or piece of glass

Floral sealant

Matt polyurethane varnish

Brushes

STEP 1

Using a damp cloth, wipe the inside and outside of the box to remove any dust or sawdust. Let the box dry or wipe again with a dry cloth.

STEP 2

Paint the box both inside and out with red paint. I used aerosol car paint, because I like the finish: new untreated wood soaks up the paint and you can still see the grain of the wood though the colour. I also prefer using aerosols as it's quicker and there are no brushes to wash. However, there is no reason why you cannot use any paint you like.

STEP 3

When the red paint is dry, lightly spray the mossy green paint into joints and corners, anywhere that dirt might settle or heavy wear might mark the box. This helps to tone down the red and makes the box look old and interesting.

STEP 4

Leave the paint to dry thoroughly and if possible, leave the lid open overnight in a well-ventilated room to get rid of as much of the paint smell as possible. Then decide on your design. With such a large project you might find it helpful to lay the flowers and leaves out on a piece of paper cut to the same size as the top or sides of the chest. When planning your chest, take into account the background colour you intend to paint the chest and the choice of larger size flowers to which you have access.

STEP 5

Once you are happy with the design, transfer it on to the chest, sticking the flowers down well but avoiding overuse of the glue or it will seep out from under the pressed material.

STEP 6

Once the flowers and leaves are well stuck on, spray with sealant. Once this has dried, apply a coat of varnish. Polyurethane varnish dries more quickly than other types, so you can apply several coats in a day. Take care not to apply too much varnish at once or you will have runs and drips that look unsightly. It may help to lay the chest on its side or back so that you are not working on a vertical surface.

STEP 7

Continue to apply the varnish until you are happy with the effect and feel that there is plenty of protection for the flowers. Alternatively, continue applying at least 20 coats or maybe even more, if you want a perfect mirror finish.

How About?

Apart from mixing paper cut-outs with the pressed flowers, you can also stencil the box and then decorate with pressed flowers. I have experimented with stencilled urns filled with pressed flowers, and stencilled terracotta pots on to a box that were then 'filled' with plants and flowers. This made a very unusual effect that has been much admired.

Rock-a-Bye Baby!

 This adorable little rocking chair looks very pretty in plain white, but the addition of wild morning glory flowers and leaves tumbling over it adds a special charm. You could do this with any number of different plants, perhaps adding the child's name or date of birth. Make sure that you apply plenty of coats of varnish, as obviously any chair intended for a child's use will have to withstand a lot of wear and tear. You can decorate any small piece of furniture in this way.

YOU WILL NEED

Cloth

Child's chair or suitable piece of furniture

Emulsion or gloss paint

Paintbrush

Transfers (optional)

Pressed wild columbine or morning glory

Tweezers

White latex adhesive

Old dinner plate or piece of glass

Floral sealant

Clear polyurethane varnish

Medium-sized brush

STEP 1

Using a damp cloth, clean the chair very thoroughly to remove any dust, grease or dirt. Then rub it over with a dry cloth so the surface is not wet. If you are renovating an old chair, make sure that the legs are not wobbly and that the chair is not infested with woodworm. Paint it with emulsion or gloss paint, adding a second coat if necessary. Leave to dry.

STEP 2

If you want to add the child's name or date of birth, now is the time to do it so that the flowers can be arranged around it. You can use paint or, if you are dubious about your freehand lettering capabilities, use letter transfers.

STEP 3

Once the name is completely dry, arrange the trails of flowers along the arms and back of the chair, over the seat and anywhere else you fancy. If you have pressed a reasonably long trail of plant material, you may have to break it into smaller pieces to get the right shape with twists and turns. You may need to add separate flowers to make the design look prettier; often the trails of morning glory are not over-endowed with blooms.

STEP 4

Stick down the flowers and leaves, gluing thoroughly but not using too much glue. Once it is dry, check for excess blobs of glue that may show later and remove them. Then spray with a coat of floral sealant.

STEP 5

Cover the whole chair with a coat of varnish. When dry, varnish it again at least eighteen to twenty times. Bear in mind that if a chair is designed for a child it is undoubtedly going to receive very hard wear and tear, so use plenty of protective layers of varnish. I found quick-drying polyurethane varnish the easiest to use. If any lumps and bumps do appear, or if you develop a run or drip in the varnish, sand lightly with fine-grade sandpaper.

How About?

The same technique can be applied to chests of drawers, small desks or occasional tables. The sky is the limit! If the flowers fade after some time and you would like a new brighter design, sand off the old design, repaint where necessary and start again.

Pretty as a Picture!

Decorating a photograph frame with pressed flowers adds charm to a photograph. You need a moderately wide frame that is fairly flat, rather than one with a complicated profile that would entail bending and possibly breaking the pressed bits and pieces. It is usually more successful to keep to a relatively simple pressed flower design as anything over-detailed can detract from the photograph. Bear your subject in mind.

YOU WILL NEED

Wide, flat photograph frame
Pressed flowers and leaves
White latex adhesive
Old dinner plate or piece of glass
Tweezers
Floral sealant
Polyurethane varnish
Brush

STEP 1

Make sure the frame is clean and dry. Then lay out the flowers and leaves to decide how you would like to arrange them. If you know which photograph you intend to frame, then it may be worth trying to match the colour of the flowers to the picture as I have done with the blue cornflowers and the colour of Emily's dress.

STEP 2

Once you have decided exactly where you want to put the flowers, glue them on carefully, using the all-over gluing method (see page 35). Take care that there are no blobs of glue visible and allow the glue to dry. Then spray the flowers with a coat of floral sealant.

STEP 3

Apply a coat of polyurethane varnish over the frame and leave to dry. It is up to you how many coats of varnish you wish to apply – but you will probably need at least six. This will not produce a really flat surface, but will protect the flowers.

How About?

Paint the frame before decorating it with flowers for a coloured background. Or you could use the language of flowers and say 'I love you' in red roses around a frame. Once I decorated a photograph frame with a gardener's favourite flowers and then presented it to her with a picture of her garden inside, which was a great success.

Decorated Dressing Table

Once you have tried a couple of small projects, why not be brave and tackle something a little larger?

This project could be made using a brand new dressing table or a really inexpensive piece of junk you have discovered. The varnishing technique is just as effective for a piece of bedroom, bathroom or sitting room furniture, but do remember, the greater the wear and tear it is likely to receive, the greater the number of coats of varnish you should apply to protect your design.

YOU WILL NEED

Dressing table or other piece of furniture
Sandpaper (optional)
Paint and paintbrush (optional)
Pressed flowers and leaves
White latex adhesive
Old dinner plate or piece of glass
Floral sealant
Quick-drying polyurethane varnish
Small brush

STEP 1

If you are decorating an old piece of furniture, sand it well, then paint or stain it with whatever colour you desire. A new piece may not need painting, just a good clean to make sure it is grease-free and dry.

STEP 2

Plan your flower design for the dressing table. If you are going to use the furniture every day, it may be easier to leave the top with a simple design and concentrate on the uprights that will not receive so much wear and tear.

STEP 3

When you are happy with your ideas, glue the flowers on to the various surfaces. When the glue has dried, spray with floral sealant.

STEP 4

Start to cover the flowers with coats of varnish. On a piece of furniture, I usually apply at least ten to fifteen coats, to ensure that they will stand up to daily use. Another means of protection would be to cover the top of the dressing table with a piece of glass. This is fairly expensive, but means the design will be safe no matter how much the dressing table is used.

How About?

Once you have completed the dressing table, how about decorating some accessories to match? You could choose the same flowers and decorate some bottles (see pages 72-73), or buy a dressing table set to decorate (see useful addresses on page 110).

$\mathcal{M}$usical Hat Box

This truly beautiful hat box is simple to copy and is such a pretty storage idea for anything from scarves to love letters! Perhaps you could find the sheet music from 'your tune' and mix it with a collection of sentimental flowers to house some of your romantic keepsakes.
You can age the paper to create a vintage effect for truly antique appeal. Old photographs, Victorian scraps or pictures of fruit and flowers would also look good with this effect.

YOU WILL NEED

Scissors
Photocopied or original sheet music
White latex adhesive
Old dinner plate or piece of glass
Papier mâché hat box
Pressed flowers (I used roses)
Tweezers
Floral sealant
Polyurethane varnish
Small brush

STEP 1

Cut up the sheet music into abstract shapes. Make some cuts diagonally across the music staves and others at different angles.

STEP 2

Using white latex adhesive, glue the music pieces to the hat box, ensuring that all the edges and corners are well-glued or they will lift when you varnish the box.

STEP 3

Glue narrow pieces of music cut to size around the rim.

STEP 4

Using tweezers, glue the flowers on to the box in groups to achieve a stronger impact.

STEP 5

Try using rose leaves as well as flowers to add a little green to the design. Once all the flowers are glued in place and the glue has had time to dry, spray the entire box with a floral sealant. This is essential unless you wish the paper to discolour to a dark tan once the varnish is applied.

STEP 6

Apply at least eight coats of varnish, allowing them to dry between applications. If you preferred, you could then apply some antique-effect varnish to achieve an antique, cracked finish. This is available from specialist paint shops and by mail-order (see page 110).

How About?

Instead of using sheet music, how about using photographs, black and white photocopies of fruit or flowers or brightly coloured Victorian scraps?

$\mathcal{A}$ Flower Chest

This tiny chest of drawers would be ideal for storing jewellery or small bits and pieces such as hair accessories and ribbons. It is gradually becoming easier to find blanks of this nature in craft shops and florists' wholesalers. A word of warning however; if you see one and think you like it, buy it immediately as you can be sure it will have gone when you return for it at a later date! These blanks are always useful.

YOU WILL NEED

Cloth

Small chest of drawers
(this one is approximately 45 cm
(18 in) high)

Selection of pressed flowers and leaves

Tweezers

White latex adhesive

Old dinner plate or piece of glass

Floral sealant

Polyurethane varnish

Small brush

STEP 1

Using a damp cloth, wipe the chest clean, both inside and out. Then dry it well.

STEP 2

Arrange your pressed flowers in position and once you are happy with the design, glue them into place. In this example, I used jasmine leaves and pink larkspur with some elderflowers.

STEP 3

Spray the flowers carefully with floral sealant. Once this is dry, apply the first coat of varnish. Let the varnish dry completely between coats and apply at least six to eight coats. Take great care that you do not apply the varnish so liberally that you manage to varnish across the drawer fronts, so that they no longer open (I must confess that I made this mistake once, so this is a note from personal experience.)

How About?

These small chests of drawers are usually made from plain unfinished wood, so there are many different ways that you can paint or decorate them before you add your flowers. An antiqued paint or crackle-glazed finish looks very effective, or you could use wood stain to give the chest an antique pine finish.

Terracotta Flower Pots

 This is a very useful project, as the pots do not take too long to make and are always a huge success as gifts.
A beautifully decorated pot makes such a difference to a house plant that you are planning to give as a present. I have not tried decorating pots to use outside, but you would certainly have to apply plenty of layers of varnish and of course avoid too much sunlight or the flowers and leaves may quickly fade.

YOU WILL NEED

Assorted small terracotta pots
Sponge (optional)
Emulsion paint, if required
Selection of pressed flowers and leaves
Tweezers
White latex adhesive
Old dinner plate or piece of glass
Floral sealant
Polyurethane varnish
Small brush

STEP 1

You can decorate the terracotta pots as they are, or you can paint them first. Sponge paint on to the pots, using two or three different colours to give extra interest to the design. Alternatively, a plain coat of white or cream paint looks great as a background. If you are giving the pots without plants inside, then I think it is important to finish them professionally inside as well. If you want to save time (but not money) use aerosol emulsion paint; this can be quickly sprayed inside the pot and gives a good even finish. It is not, however, very cost-effective.

STEP 2

Once you have painted your pot, then you can apply the flowers. Glue them on well with the latex adhesive and allow the glue to dry. When the glue is quite dry, spray with floral sealant.

STEP 3

Apply several coats of polyurethane varnish, allowing the varnish to dry completely between coats.

How About?

After decorating one pot, you could try a matching set of plant pots in various sizes, or a gift set of three pots decorated with herbs and planted up for the kitchen windowsill: match the herb on the outside of the pot to the plant inside. Or simply decorate the pots with a small posy of herbs and paint a small bow with a trailing ribbon to finish the design.

Flowered Vase

This beautiful vase manages to deceive everyone who sees it – there is no way anyone would guess it was made from rather dull papier mâché. There are so many different papier mâché objects available today that a similar technique can be used to disguise many different objects. The key is patience and many different layers and colours of paint. It is important to make the inside look well-finished, thus adding the final professional touch.

YOU WILL NEED

Cloth
Blank papier mâché vase
Paint in at least three colours, one light and two dark
Paintbrush
Sponges
Pressed flowers and leaves
Tweezers
White latex adhesive
Old dinner plate or piece of glass
Floral sealant
Polyurethane varnish
Small brush

STEP 1

Dust the papier mâché vase inside and out to remove dirt or loose paper. Paint the vase a pale colour, such as white or cream. I used an aerosol paint to finish the inside; if making this as a gift, it is important that it looks well-finished.

STEP 2

Sponge different colours on to the pale base; I used yellow and maroon. By using several colours you can achieve the necessary depth to make the vase look more substantial than it really is.

STEP 3

Once you are satisfied with the sponging, leave to dry. Then glue on your choice of flowers and leaves. I used *Helleborus orientalis* flowers and herb robert leaves.

STEP 4

Make sure the flowers are evenly spaced and are well stuck down. Then spray the whole vase with floral sealant.

STEP 5

Once the sealant is dry, apply the first coat of varnish. You will need to apply at least three or four coats, depending on how smooth you want the surface to be. For a really good mirror finish, you will need many more. Allow each coat to dry before further applications.

How About?

The paint treatments can be varied to give a totally different look. You could use a crackle finish for an older look or use pressed flowers and plants to create a collage design or picture on the vase. Patterns are easier to create on a large surface area like this, but it depends what you enjoy creating the most.

Pretty Papier Mâché Pencil Box

This is another papier mâché project that would make a lovely present for a young schoolgirl – or even an adult who likes to write. There are many pretty pencils that you could buy to put inside this pencil case, perhaps in colours to tone with the paint effect that you choose. For a young boy, you could use plant material to make a cartoon picture of a duck, a mouse or even a small landscape, to make the finished effect less feminine.

YOU WILL NEED

Papier mâché pencil box
Sponges or brushes
Paint
Selection of pressed flowers and leaves
Tweezers
White latex adhesive
Old dinner plate or piece of glass
Floral sealant
Polyurethane varnish
Small brush

STEP 1

Sponge or spray the pencil box with a base colour of paint; I chose a light base so that I could add various darker colours on top.

STEP 2

Once the base coat is dry, begin to sponge the secondary colours on to the box. You need several colours to achieve the interesting effect pictured here. Plain colours can look just as effective as sponged colours, but may need several coats.

STEP 3

Finish sponging the other colours on to the box. Once you are happy with the outside of the box, check the inside and make sure that this also looks well-finished.

STEP 4

Arrange a spray of flowers along the top of the box; I used jasmine leaves and pink larkspur. Take care the flowers do not cover the hinged area at the back of the box, or they may be damaged by constant opening and shutting of the box.

STEP 5

Glue the flowers well and, once the glue is dry, spray with floral sealant. Varnish the whole box, especially over the flowers, applying at least six to eight coats. Be sure to allow the varnish to dry completely between each coat.

Decorated Bottles

These pretty bottles started life as plain green recycled glass, which is widely available and relatively inexpensive. You will also find many pretty bottles used as packaging, especially for wine and cider vinegar or oils. These look very elegant when decorated.

YOU WILL NEED

Selection of glass bottles

Sponges

Glass paints

White latex adhesive

Old dinner plate or piece of glass

Selection of flowers and leaves

Tweezers

Floral sealant

Varnish

Small brush

STEP 1

To add interest to the bottles, sponge them with paints especially designed for use on glass. The two colours were a strong mid-blue and a mossy green. These mingle together beautifully to create a watery effect.

STEP 2

Once the paint has dried, which it does pretty quickly, glue your choice of flowers and leaves on to the front and back of the bottle. Allow the glue to dry, then spray with floral sealant.

STEP 3

Apply a coat of varnish. I used the varnish supplied with the glass paints, so that it was compatible with the paint. Apply at least two or three coats and ensure that all the flowers are well covered.

How About?

Decorating glassware opens a whole new world of possibilities. Glass vases and ornaments would look lovely decorated with pressed flowers, and even a sheet of glass could be decorated and then framed. You could fill the bottles with fragrant bath salts or cologne, to make really elegant gifts that will be cherished.

Rosy Jug

 This jug is another papier mâché object that looks wonderful when it has been decorated, but seems very plain and boring beforehand. Although I have painted this one a plain colour with a little darker shading for interest, you could paint it in stripes or patterns to give a different effect.

YOU WILL NEED

Papier mâché jug

Sponges or brushes

Paints

White latex adhesive

Old dinner plate or piece of glass

Selection of pressed flowers and leaves

Tweezers

Floral sealant

Polyurethane varnish

Small brush

STEP 1

Spray, sponge or brush a base coat of paint over the jug. I used red to give a strong dark background, so that the pale pink roses show up to best advantage.

STEP 2

Once the base coat is dry, sponge on a couple of contrasting colours; I used a touch of purple and green, very lightly, just to add some shading. Allow to dry thoroughly.

STEP 3

Glue the flowers and leaves on carefully and, if necessary, hold them in position until the glue firms up. Gluing flowers on to a curved surface can be a little difficult as they sometimes refuse to stay in position and curl up. When the glue is dry, spray with floral sealant.

STEP 4

Apply several layers of varnish over the jug. As the basic jug is made from papier mâché, it is best to use it for dried flowers. However, if you wish to use it for fresh flowers, then place a small jam jar of water inside and arrange the flowers in that.

How About?

A whole co-ordinating display could be made by buying some inexpensive papier mâché pieces – a bowl, jug, and vases – and painting them all the same colour. You could then decorate them with various flower arrangements that either matched or co-ordinated, and the whole collection would only cost a reasonable amount.

CHAPTER 6

Flowers under Glass

The most popular and perhaps the most traditional way to display pressed flowers is by protecting them under a sheet of glass. The glass can be clear, non-reflective or even museum standard with special ultraviolet filters. In my opinion the type of glass does not make any difference to the colour fastness of the flowers, but I know others feel differently. The main causes of fading seem to be strong light (of any variety) and exposure to the air. If the picture is completely airtight, then the colour of the flowers lasts much longer than if exposed to the elements. Having conducted many experiments with all the different glass varieties, the flowers seemed to fade at the same speed when put in strong sunlight, so I always use good-quality clear float glass, which enhances the picture rather than detracting from it as I feel the non-reflective glass does. However, this is always a personal choice and when you are making your pictures you must consider all the alternatives and decide which effect you prefer.

The picture must be planned as a whole. The floral design is of paramount importance, but to achieve a really pleasing effect, you must think carefully about the background and the frame. I usually think of the type of picture I want to make and plan the flowers first, although not in any great detail. Having decided on the rough contents of the picture, I then choose a background, either card, paper or fabric. Once this combination has been sorted out, I then take the backing and the flowers (in their packets) to a framer and decide on a size. Alternatively, I work the other way round and create the picture first and then transport it to a framer to choose the frame.

There are many different choices when you come to frame your picture; indeed, the choice of frame is just as crucial as the choice of each flower and leaf in the design. Your work is worthy of care when you frame it. This does not mean that it is essential to spend huge amounts of money on a frame; an old one that you already have may well be a fabulous match for the picture. But think it through before making your choice. Sometimes a frame with just a tinge of blue will transform a picture by bringing out a pale blue flower that would become totally invisible in a bright tan-coloured wooden frame. A vastly ornate gilded frame may completely overpower a pretty wildflower design where a narrow pine frame could be just the thing.

Small pressed flower pictures are a very versatile gift idea. You could take a tiny picture as a present for your hostess when you go to dinner or for the weekend or you can make wonderful creations as birthday, Christmas or wedding presents. I have never known anything flowery to be unappreciated in the same way that no one is likely to say 'no, thank you' if you offer them a bunch of fresh flowers.

Merry Christmas

The idea for this picture came to me when I spotted the wonderful wrapping paper that I have used as a background. I often make table centre decorations with small poinsettias and some foliage from the garden and this is a recreation of that type of seasonal floral display. You could include other festive items, such as pine foliage and mistletoe (although the berries are not very successful) in the arrangement.

YOU WILL NEED

Masking tape, 1.5 cm (⅝ in) and 4 cm (1½ in) wide

Sheet of wrapping paper

Cream mount, cut with an oval aperture about 50 x 40 cm (20 x 16 in)

Scissors

Frame with glass and a hardboard back, with hanger attached, about 60 x 50 cm (24 x 20 in)

Piece of foam, 45 x 35 cm (18 x 14 in) and about 1.5 cm (⅝ in) thick

Pressed poinsettia bracts, ivy trails and sprays of euonymous leaves and holly

Tweezers

White latex adhesive

Tapestry needle

Framing gun, or hammer and nails

Thick paper (optional)

STEP 1

Using the narrow masking tape, attach the sheet of wrapping paper to the back of the mount, trimming the paper slightly smaller than the outside measurement of the mount.

STEP 2

Fix the paper on to the mount so that it is tightly stretched across the oval aperture. Trim any ends of tape that are left.

STEP 3

Place the piece of hardboard on a table, with the hanger facing down. Put the foam on top and then place the mount on top of the foam.

STEP 4

Lay out the leaves and poinsettias. I find it easiest to place the green bracts from the poinsettia in position first. As the red bracts tend to disappear against the red paper backing, the green leaves are essential as a contrast. Once you have the focal points of your poinsettias started, add the red bracts and then start to pad out the display with single holly leaves and some sprays of variegated euonymous leaves.

STEP 5

Trail the ivy over the edge of the mount to add interest to the picture. Once you are happy with the arrangement, try to leave it for a short while. When you look at it again, you will be able to be much more objective about your work.

STEP 6

Once you are satisfied with your work, fix the flowers and leaves with a small amount of latex adhesive. Do not remove the flowers from the picture, just use a tapestry needle to apply the glue, sliding it under the petals and leaves to glue them down. Once the picture is framed, the glass will hold the flowers in position, so this is just to make the framing process a little easier.

STEP 7

Clean the glass well and place it over the design. Lay the frame on top and then compress the whole package into the frame and turn it over. Once it is upside down, you can fix the hardboard into the frame using a framing gun or framer's staple gun. Alternatively, hammer in nails at 2.5 cm (1 in) intervals. If none of these methods is possible, then choose a photograph frame with the pliable clips that can be bent over to keep the frame closed.

STEP 8

Most importantly, remember to seal the back well at this stage. The most attractive way to seal the back is to cover it completely with thick paper. Cut some brown paper or plain coloured paper to size (or more of the pretty wrapping paper), apply some glue around the edge of the frame and carefully press the paper down.

A quicker and easier alternative is to use 4 cm (1½ in) wide masking tape and tape across the crack between the hardboard and the frame, trimming the tape neatly at the corners.

How About?

Try using short lengths of cream ribbon as candles with trimmed yellow lily petals for the flame. Alternatively, tartan ribbons or a few mock presents could be included among the greenery; to make mock presents, cut small rectangles of attractive wrapping paper and decorate them with some contrasting narrow gold ribbon.

Helleborus Orientalis

Botanical Picture

*I have always been fascinated by the Victorian botanical prints that depict a plant in
the various stages of growth and I thought it would be fun to make a pressed flower version.
The hellebore is one of my favourite plants, it presses beautifully and retains its colour
well, so this made an excellent choice. You could also do a much smaller version with forget-me-nots
or snowdrops. Another botanical approach would be to frame a collection of ten different varieties of ivy
or any plant of which you have several different types. Add the botanical names if you wish.*

YOU WILL NEED

Pressed plant material

Backing material or paper

Scissors

Suitable frame with glass and
hardboard back, with hanger attached,
about 50 x 40cm (20 x 16in)

Thin foam, cut to about 47 x 37cm
(18¾ x 14¾in), and approximately
1cm (½in) thick

Brown pen (optional)

White latex adhesive

Large tapestry needle

Framing gun, or hammer and nails

Thick paper (optional)

Masking tape, 4cm (1½in) wide

STEP 1

Press as many different bits and
pieces of the plant as you can. I
used small pieces of the root, buds,
open flowers and seedlings. If you
are pressing pieces of root, take care
to make them as fine as possible or
they may cause problems with
creasing or bulges when you come
to frame the picture.

STEP 2

Choose a suitable backing; you
could use something like hessian
for a textured effect, or plain cream
silk which could be aged with tea or
coffee. I used a modern paper
printed to look like parchment; you
could also achieve wonderful effects
with handmade papers, which are
available in so many subtle colours
and finishes. Cut your backing to
the size of the glass.

STEP 3

Lay the hardboard on a table with
the hanger facing downwards. Lay
the foam on top and then your
choice of backing on top of that.
Experiment with the different
pieces of pressed plant material,
placing them in various positions
until you are pleased with the
overall effect.

STEP 4

Once you feel that the balance is
right, add the name of the plant if
you wish. I used a brown pen for
this, as black might have been a
little overpowering. Then, using
latex adhesive and a large tapestry
needle, place a little glue under all
the flowers, leaves and roots so that
they won't move while you are
framing the design.

STEP 5

When the glue is dry, clean the glass
well and place it over the picture.
Place the frame over the top and
compress all the contents. Turn
over carefully and fix the hardboard
into the frame using a framing gun
or by hammering in nails at 2.5cm
(1in) intervals.

STEP 6

Seal the back of the picture by
covering it completely with sturdy
paper, or by using 4cm (1½in)
wide masking tape to cover the
crack between the hardboard and
the frame.

How About?

*There are many choices of plants that
could lend themselves to this
treatment. Roses look lovely in
various stages and small spring bulbs
could be used with a section of
the bulb included. Dramatic parrot
tulips would make a stunning
botanical picture.*

Summer Hanging Basket

One of the happiest memories I have of summer is of beautiful hanging baskets of flowers. I love having really full containers on patios and around our back door. This picture keeps the memory alive through the winter and is fun to make. You can use a wide range of pressed summer bedding plants, and you will find there is no need to create a wire container as the foliage usually covers this. If necessary, supplement with some trailing ivy to fill any gaps.

YOU WILL NEED

Mount

Silk fabric

Masking tape, 1.5 cm (⅝ in) and 4 cm (1½ in) wide

Suitable frame with glass and hardboard back, with hanger attached, approximately 30 x 30 cm (12 x 12 in)

Foam, cut to about 27 x 27 cm (10¾ x 10¾ in), and 1.5 cm (⅝ in) thick

3 pieces of green-covered florist's wire

Selection of pressed summer bedding plants, including pansies and some pressed green reindeer moss

White latex adhesive

Tapestry needle

Framing gun, or hammer and nails

STEP 1

Prepare the mount by stretching the silk across the back of the circular aperture and fixing with narrow masking tape. The silk must be taut or it will wrinkle later. Place the hardboard on a table top with the hanger facing downwards, and cover with the foam, then place the mount on top.

STEP 2

Carefully position the three green pieces of wire, trimming them down a little if necessary. They can be slipped under the mount to hold them in position. Put a large pansy and some buds at the top of the basket and place some leaves around the base of the basket where the container would be.

STEP 3

Add some light, bright flowers to the design. I have used white daisies as they give a lovely contrast to the darker flowers and foliage. Notice that I have used some buds and foliage as well as daisy flowers. This gives a much more realistic feel to the design.

STEP 4

Add some trailing plants, as these help to give body and depth to the basket. I have used trailing lobelia, which keeps its colour beautifully, and some trailing ivy. Variegated ivy does not press very well in the traditional way but by using the microwave it retains a wonderful colour and gives good contrast.

STEP 5

Fill up the basket area with small pieces of pressed moss. Commercially preserved reindeer moss can be pressed and looks very effective. You could use other varieties if you prefer.

STEP 6

Finally, add some more large flowers to star in the design. I love pansies and they come out a beautiful sparkling colour when pressed by microwave. Glue the components down well, using a tapestry needle to slide a little glue under every flower and leaf.

STEP 7

Place the glass over the top and compress the contents. Turn the whole 'sandwich' over and fix the hardboard into the frame by using a framing gun, or by hammering nails into the back at 2.5 cm (1 in) intervals. Then tape over the crack between the hardboard and the frame with 4 cm (1½ in) wide masking tape.

How About?

There are so many other flowers that would look stunning used in a design like this. Fuchsias immediately spring to mind. A large basket filled to overflowing with tiny fuchsias would look wonderful. You could also use many other summer plants or perhaps try a winter hanging-basket with ivy, heather and other foliage.

Secret Garden

This design, intended to resemble a small piece of a herbaceous border, uses a great many flowers and leaves, but looks very effective and is fun to plan. You could either collect flowers from your own garden especially for this design, or use some that you already have in stock. I have made several presents for friends using a selection of flowers from their own gardens, which have proved very successful gifts. You will need plenty of leaves as a base for the 'border'.

Cream silk measuring about 48 x 38cm (19¼ x 15¼in)

Mount (either a single colour or a double mount as used here)

Masking tape, 1.5cm (⅝in) and 4cm (1½in) wide

Suitable frame with glass and back, with a hanger attached, measuring 50 x 40cm (20 x 16in)

Piece of foam, measuring about 48 x 38cm (19¼ x 15¼in), and 12mm (½in) thick

Pressed flowers and leaves

White latex adhesive

Tapestry needle

Framing gun, or hammer and nails

STEP 1

Stretch the silk across the back of the mount and secure with the narrow masking tape. Make sure that the silk is taut and free from wrinkles.

STEP 2

Place the hardboard back on a table with the picture hanger facing downwards, then place the foam over the top. Lay the mount on top of this and you are now ready for the flowers and leaves.

STEP 3

Begin by placing all the tall background flowers or leaves in position. I used some pieces of eucalyptus on the left of the design, then polygonum, monkshood and foliage. Leave a little room for the sky, but not too much.

STEP 4

Begin to fill in the base with larger flowers. Pretend that you are planting them in a bed and place them in clumps, rather than scattering them randomly.

STEP 5

Make sure that there are plenty of leaves tucked between the lower flowers to make a firm base for the 'flowerbed', and then tuck some smaller feathery bits and pieces into the design to make sure it really looks like a flowerbed in full summer bloom.

STEP 6

Once you are happy with the picture, clean the glass carefully and place over the top of the design. Have a short break and come back to the picture to enable you to see the design more objectively.

STEP 7

Remove the glass and carefully glue down the flowers and leaves by sliding a tapestry needle dipped in glue under each one.

STEP 8

Once everything is well glued – with no excess glue visible – replace the glass over the design. Then put the frame over the glass and compress the contents well. Turn it over and place on a table top. Fix in the backing by pressing firmly and securing with a framing gun, or by hammering in nails at 2.5cm (1in) intervals. Tape the back of the frame with the wide masking tape to prevent any damp or dust getting into the picture.

How About?

You could collect suitable flowers and leaves throughout the seasons, and make a lovely set of pictures showing the four seasons in your garden or a friend's. The same design also works well with a collection of woodland material, or grasses and wildflowers.

Pressed Wedding Bouquet

 The bouquet is such a central feature of any wedding that many people want to keep it as a souvenir of their day. This can be achieved in many different ways, but one of the most successful is to press the flowers beautifully in the microwave, so ensuring excellent colour retention, then to recreate them in the shape of the original bouquet. You can also dry the flowers and make them into a picture or pot pourri. You can press the flowers traditionally or you can freeze dry them, but microwave pressing would be my choice. You will find more information about pressing difficult flowers like these stargazer lilies and orchids in the techniques section (see pages 32 and 28).

YOU WILL NEED

Pressed flowers from the bouquet

Silk, cut to 57 x 47 cm (22¾ x 18¾ in)

Masking tape, 1.5 cm (⅝ in) and 4 cm (1½ in) wide

Mount to tone with both the frame and the flowers

Suitable frame with glass and hardboard back, with hanger attached, about 60 x 50 cm (24 x 20 in)

Foam, cut to 57 x 47 cm (22¾ x 18¾ in)

Tweezers

White latex adhesive

Tapestry needle

Framing gun, or hammer and nails

STEP 1

If the design you are trying to recreate is a tied bunch, as this one was, make sure that you have remembered to press some of the stalks from the bouquet – it's easy to forget. Tape the silk across the back of the mount so that it is taut.

STEP 2

Place the hardboard back on a table with the picture hanger facing downwards, then place the foam over the top. Turn the mount the right way round and lay this on top.

STEP 3

Place the stems in position on the silk and then add the largest flowers, in this case the lilies.

STEP 4

Fill in the outline a little with rosebuds and plenty of rose leaves. Then add the delphiniums and the variegated foliage. Keep looking at the shape to check the design is working. I usually refer back to a photo of the original bouquet.

STEP 5

Cover the top of the stalks with plenty of rose leaves; this not only fills the picture but also disguises the ends of the stalks. Add to the daintiness of the outline by using plenty of gypsophila.

STEP 6

Place the three mini gerbera flowers into the design. Move them around until you find the best positioning. Don't worry if the odd petal or two becomes loose. When your design is complete, you can just glue them back on to the centre of the flower and it will not show.

STEP 7

Check the picture well to make sure that the balance is right and that you have some pretty contrasts, like a spray of gypsophila against a green rose leaf.

STEP 8

Then glue down all the component flowers and leaves in the picture by applying a little latex adhesive to the back of each; using a tapestry needle, taking care not to leave any excess glue visible.

STEP 9

Clean the glass carefully to remove any smears or dust and place it over the top of the design. Put the frame over the glass and compress the contents. Then turn the entire assembly over and place on a table top. Fix in the backing by pressing firmly and securing with a framing gun, or by hammering in small panel pins at 2.5 cm (1 in) intervals. Tape the back of the frame with the wide masking tape to prevent damp or dust getting into the picture.

How About?

If there are any flowers left over, you could also make some souvenir pictures for other members of the family. Often a very full wedding bouquet will produce many more flowers than you will need to complete a medium- to large-sized picture. Try some varying designs.

You could also add to the picture the names of the bride and groom or the date of the wedding, or sprinkle some confetti over the bouquet. Instead of using a plain piece of silk, you could ask for a small piece of the fabric used for the bride's gown, or one of the bridesmaid's dresses.

Mother's Corsage Memento

It's not just the bride who wants to keep a memory of the happy day – the bride's mother is often as sentimental about the day as the couple themselves. This uses the flowers in her corsage to make a pretty keepsake. Keep the size of the corsage in mind when choosing a frame – a large corsage will not make a picture that will fit into a tiny brooch-sized frame. The opposite also applies – don't try to make a large picture using only a very few flowers, unless you are happy to add some of the church or reception flowers to boost the supplies.

YOU WILL NEED

Oval frame with glass and hardboard back, with hanger attached, measuring 25 x 20 cm (10 x 8 in)

Foam or wadding, cut to the same size

Silk or other fabric, cut to the same size

Pressed flowers and leaves

Tweezers

White latex adhesive

Tapestry needle

Framing gun, or hammer and nails

Masking tape, 4 cm (1½ in) wide

STEP 1

The colour scheme chosen for this wedding was mauve and pink. The Singapore orchids press particularly well in the microwave, as do the pale pink roses. Lay the back of the frame on a table top with the hanger facing downwards, then place the foam or wadding on top and cover with a piece of silk. Place the oval frame over the piece of silk. This will give you a framework to stay within and will make sure that the finished picture is neither too big nor too small.

STEP 2

Remembering the style of the corsage (refer to a picture if necessary), place the rose leaves on the silk. Then add a few jasmine leaves and a little gypsophila.

STEP 3

Place some of the pink rosebuds at the top and bottom of the picture, then add the orchids. Check the outside edge of the picture; the shape should be about right by now. Remove the frame.

STEP 4

Next, place a fully-opened rose in position (for details on how to make these up see the techniques section, page 13). Move the large rose around to make sure it is the right size and shape to fill the gap in your corsage. Condense the petals a little if you have made it too big.

STEP 5

Look carefully at the picture and add a little more foliage and gypsophila until you feel happy with the design. Glue down all the flowers and leaves with the needle dipped in glue.

STEP 6

Clean the glass carefully and place it over the top of the design. Put the frame over the glass and compress the contents. Then turn it over and place on a table top. Fix in the backing by pressing firmly and secure in place with a framing gun, or by hammering in nails at 2.5 cm (1 in) intervals. Tape the back of the frame with the wide masking tape to prevent damp or dust getting into the picture.

How About?

You could make a matching pair of oval pictures for the bride's mother and father, by pressing the father's buttonhole and mother's corsage. Any elderly members of the family who were unable to attend the wedding could perhaps have a small picture made from flowers at the reception or church.

New Baby Flowers

The most memorable times in a mother's life have to be the births of her children. I have two girls and can remember those moments as though they happened yesterday. Hopefully you will have a supportive partner who will bring you some special flowers. Now, I realize that, as a brand new mother, pressing some flowers in the microwave may not be high on your agenda of urgent priorities, but maybe a granny or friend of the family could oblige. The actual picture can be made up at a later date, when the new baby allows you some free time!

YOU WILL NEED

Silk or thin cotton fabric

Card mount with an oval aperture, about 20 x 16cm (8 x 6¾in)

Masking tape, 1.5 cm (⅝in) and 4cm (1½in) wide

Frame with glass and a hardboard back, with hanger, about 30 x 25cm (12 x 10in)

Foam, cut to a slightly smaller size

Photograph of your new arrival

Favourite new baby greetings cards

Scissors

Pressed flowers (which keep well providing they are kept airtight, dry and in the dark)

Tweezers

Ribbon (optional)

White latex adhesive

Tapestry needle

Framing gun, or hammer and nails

STEP 1

Collect all your treasures together. You may have more mementoes that you wish to include, which may mean using a larger frame or showing less of the mount. Stretch the fabric across the back of the mount and make sure it is taut; tape to secure. Place the hardboard back of the frame on the table top so that the hanger is facing downwards; place the foam on top and cover with the mount, the right way up.

STEP 2

Play around with the photograph and cards until you find an arrangement that pleases you. I have cut the motifs out of the cards to give a softer line.

STEP 3

Decide how big the spray of flowers is going to be and place the longest and widest pieces in position. Concentrate on the outside of the bunch rather than the middle which can follow later.

STEP 4

Add some flowers and leaves to the centre of the design to fill it out. Make sure the spray has plenty of interest. Remember to press small pieces of foliage to go with the flowers and leaves. You may like to use a ribbon in the design. Using a tapestry needle and latex adhesive, carefully glue down all the parts of the picture so that nothing moves when you frame it.

STEP 5

Clean the glass carefully and place it over the top of the design. Put the frame over the glass and compress the contents. Then turn it over and place on a table top. Fix in the backing by pressing firmly and secure the backing in place with a framing gun, or by hammering in nails at 2.5 cm (1 in) intervals. Tape the back of the frame with the wide masking tape to prevent damp or dust getting into the picture.

How About?

This would make a lovely present for a new mum; if you can't persuade her to part with the actual flowers, you could buy some similar ones to recreate the bouquet.

Bridal Headdress

Much is always made of pressing the bride's bouquet – but many people like to throw their bouquet in the traditional manner or take it as a gift to a relative who couldn't attend the wedding. This alternative of pressing the bridal headdress could make just as pretty a memory; you could also use a bridesmaid's headdress. Remember to save leftover fabric from the wedding dresses, as it makes an attractive background to your picture.

YOU WILL NEED

Fabric, cut to a slightly smaller size than the aperture

Mount with a circular aperture

Masking tape, 1.5 cm (⅝ in) and 4 cm (1½ in) wide

Frame with glass and a hardboard back, with hanger, approximately 33 cm (13¼ in) square

Foam, cut to a slightly smaller size

Pressed flowers and foliage

Tweezers

White latex adhesive

Tapestry neeedle

Framing gun, or hammer and nails

STEP 1

Stretch the fabric across the back of the mount and secure with the narrow tape. I used a piece of the bridesmaid's dress fabric. Place the hardboard back of the frame on the table top with the hanger facing downwards and cover with the foam. Then place the mount the right way up on top.

STEP 2

Start laying out the foliage that will form the basic shape of the design. Remember that the leaves must be visible on the inside of the headdress as well as the outer edge.

STEP 3

Place the large orchids in position. Any large or awkwardly-shaped flowers should go into a design as early as possible, while there is still plenty of space to manoeuvre them. Then put in place the pale blue delphiniums.

STEP 4

Add the carnations and then fill all the gaps and lighten the edges of the design with lots of little violets. These press beautifully in the microwave, retaining full colour.

STEP 5

Once you are happy with the effect of your picture, glue down the flowers and leaves using latex adhesive and a tapestry needle.

STEP 6

Clean the glass carefully and place it over the top of the design. Put the frame over the glass and compress the contents. Then turn it over and place on a table top. Fix in the backing by pressing firmly and secure it with a framing gun, or by hammering in nails at 2.5 cm (1 in) intervals. Tape the back of the frame with the wide masking tape to prevent damp or dust getting into the picture.

How About?

This design can obviously be used for an everyday picture – the circular wreath style lends itself to many different flowers and settings. You could make one with mixed summer flowers, or make a very traditional Christmas ring.

Houseplant Display

I love working with pressed flowers, dried flowers, fresh flowers and even silk flowers. But I have to admit that houseplants are not my forte. If I am given a new plant, I am always thrilled to bits, and yet it rarely lasts beyond the first week or so. I then pass it on to a friend or my mother and within weeks it looks wonderful again. I felt this picture would give me the satisfaction of a stunning group of plants without the watering!

YOU WILL NEED

Silk, cut slightly smaller than the mount

Mount (I chose a double mount with a tiny edge of terracotta showing to match the pots)

Masking tape, 1.5 cm (⅝ in) and 4 cm (⅝ in) wide

Frame with glass and a hardboard back, with hanger attached, about 60 x 50 cm (24 x 20 in)

Foam, cut slightly smaller than the mount

Handmade, textured paper in a terracotta shade

Scissors

Selection of pressed houseplant flowers and foliage

Tweezers

White latex adhesive

Tapestry needle

Framing gun, or hammer and nails

STEP 1

Stretch the silk across the back of the mount and secure with the narrow masking tape. Place the hardboard back of the frame on the table top so the hanger faces downwards and cover with foam, then put the mount on top.

STEP 2

Cut out many different sizes and shapes of terracotta pot from the sheet of handmade paper. Position them on the silk, with the largest ones at the back. Start to fill the pots with plants.

STEP 3

Having filled the largest pots at the back, progress further forward in the display. Try to have a contrast of leaf shape or colour, where possible. The spider plant and the palm have spiky leaves, so make sure that these strong shapes show up well.

STEP 4

Fill the pots at the front with small cyclamen, or any other flower from an indoor plant. Although you can make a picture containing only foliage plants, a few flowers add a very pretty focal point.

STEP 5

Add plenty of variegated leaves, for colour and contrast. Make sure that every plant is visible and is surrounded by others that contrast or otherwise show it off beautifully.

STEP 6

It may take some time to fiddle with all the small components involved in this picture but the end result is well worth it. When you are finally satisfied with the display, glue it down securely using latex adhesive and a tapestry needle, and cover it with the glass.

STEP 7

Clean the glass carefully and place it over the top of the design. Put the frame over the glass and compress the contents. Then turn it over and place on a table top. Fix in the backing by pressing firmly and secure in place with a framing gun, or by hammering in nails at 2.5 cm (1 in) intervals. Tape the back of the frame with the wide masking tape to prevent damp or dust getting into the picture.

How About?

A similar approach could be used to make a picture representing a greenhouse display or a terrarium. A much more colourful effect can be obtained by using a few bright flowers among the greenery. Another great success I had was a picture representing a friend's collection of orchid plants – I definitely would never have kept them alive.

Flowers in front of a Window

The idea for this project came when I was racking my brains for something new, different and exciting to do with pressed flowers. There are many ways of combining flowers with printed material and fabrics, and this suggestion came to mind. The poster at the rear advertises the idyllic weather in Torquay (in Devon, England); however, I have to admit that as I look out of my window now the Devon skies are far from idyllic. This project will keep you going until summer comes again, and this idea opens the way for many other variations on a theme.

YOU WILL NEED

Pretty poster of an outdoor scene

Mount cut by a professional picture framer to represent an arched window

Masking tape, 1.5 cm (⅝ in) and 4 cm (1½ in) wide

Frame with glass and hardboard back, with hanger attached, about 40 x 30 cm (16 x 12 in)

Foam, slightly smaller than the mount

Sheet of paper for the vase

Scissors

Pressed flowers and leaves

Tweezers

White latex adhesive

Tapestry needle

Framing gun, or hammer and nails

STEP 1

Hold the poster behind the window aperture in the mount and move it around until you find the best section to show once the design is finished. Tape it into position on the back of the mount with the narrow tape. Place the hardboard back of the frame on a table top so that the hanger faces downwards; cover with the foam, then place the mount on top.

STEP 2

Cut a vase from the sheet of paper. The type I used was a soft handmade paper from Japan with natural shading in it; this adds to the interest in the picture. Alternatively, you could use a piece of wrapping paper and have a decorated vase.

STEP 3

Arrange the large leaves and some of the outer flowers in place. You could choose a strong mix of ingredients; I blended two very similar, gentle colours, the parrot tulips and alstroemeria flowers, as I felt the strong blue sky was so bright that it needed soft colours to balance it out.

STEP 4

Fill in the centre of the flower arrangement and place the glass over the finished design. I found it best to leave this design overnight to see in the morning whether it needed any alterations. When you look objectively at a picture you can often spot things that you might not notice before. Then carefully glue the flowers and leaves down using latex adhesive and a tapestry needle.

STEP 5

Clean the glass carefully and place it over the top of the design. Put the frame over the glass and compress the contents. Then turn it over and place on a table top. Fix in the backing by pressing firmly and secure the backing in place with a framing gun, or by hammering in nails at 2.5 cm (1 in) intervals. Tape the back of the frame with the wide masking tape to prevent damp or dust getting into the picture.

How About?

You could use a pretty picture of a country cottage and the garden in front of it. In this instance the flowers are inside and the poster outside, but this could easily be reversed and the picture could be the inside of a house and the mount could represent the walls. You could then decorate it with trailing ivy or beautifully-pressed wisteria (it takes ages pressing it flower by flower but it works well). I hope this inspires you to try something a little out of the ordinary.

Microwave Pressing Records

Use these pages to keep a record of your microwave pressing. It is well worth taking the time to do this after each session, as you will find accurate notes invaluable the next time you want to press a particular flower. (See page 29 for further information.)

FLOWERS	PRESSING TIME	NOTES

FLOWERS	PRESSING TIME	NOTES

FLOWERS	PRESSING TIME	NOTES

FLOWERS	PRESSING TIME	NOTES

FLOWERS	PRESSING TIME	NOTES

FLOWERS	PRESSING TIME	NOTES

ACKNOWLEDGEMENTS

Above all I must thank Sandy Price for her help with all the pressing for this book ... although she knows how invaluable her help is, it's nice to have it acknowledged for a change!

I would also like to thank Kit for the design of the book and Sheila at Aurum for helping to organize this project so well. A book is always a joint effort and I am grateful to all those who have helped, organized and sorted everything for this pressed flower manual.

USEFUL ADDRESSES

The Painted Finish
Unit 6, Hatton Country World, Hatton, Nr Warwick CV35 8XA
Antique-effect varnish

Impress Flowers
Slough Farm, Westhall, Suffolk IP19 8RN
Greetings card blanks and laminating film

Framecraft Miniatures Ltd
372–376 Summer Lane, Hockley, Birmingham B19 3QA
Silver and gilt dressing table sets

Index